Killing SELF

Billy G. Wilson
319 Coyote Canyon
Shirley, Ar 72153

2018

Killing SELF

BILLY G. WILSON

iUniverse®

KILLING SELF

iUniverse books may be ordered through booksellers or by contacting:

iUniverse
1663 Liberty Drive
Bloomington, IN 47403
www.iuniverse.com
1-800-Authors (1-800-288-4677)

ISBN: 978-1-4917-3719-4 (sc)
ISBN: 978-1-4917-3718-7 (e)

Library of Congress Control Number: 2014913006

Printed in the United States of America.

iUniverse rev. date: 07/17/2014

31/14/14

Don

CONTENTS

PREFACE

I am a strait forward, stand up type of person always meeting my opponent strait up face to face. I have always lived my life in that matter and believed the Word of God is the truth, the whole truth, and nothing but the truth. That is why this country used to swear people into court with their hand on the Bible and swear by it. Of course man is much smarter than that now. (He thinks!) I have wrote this book with the same spirit and am very confident that the Spirit of God had great influence on the writing of every word of it including telling me before the start, to writing it.

After all that studying to get everything I wrote correct and plain from the Word of God as it will affirm it, I have developed a mindset that I can read any verse in the Bible and preach a sermon from it with the help of God, anytime, anywhere. I named my book *Killing Self* of course from Jesus making it plain that self has no place to approach Jesus and Paul's reference to us that are baptized into Jesus's death are dead and resurrected into the spirit of Christ Jesus. Only the spirit side of the man can receive this.

It's my intent to make this book a great learning investment worth every effort to anyone who desires to learn and experience the very Spirit of the one who created all this.

CHAPTER 1

Smarter Than God People

In the beginning means the creation of heaven and the earth, not the beginning of God or anything about him. God's dwelling place is not anywhere inside the heaven and earth that he created for man and all the creatures that he created to dwell in his creation. It was not created big enough to contain him, not the heaven and the earth combined. His dwelling place is completely outside our entire creation.

The Apostle Paul is the only one I see that wrote anything much about God's dwelling place. I believe he referred to it as the third heaven. He told us very little about it, mostly just that it existed, and lived under a completely different set of laws. If you cannot grasp that and that frame of mind, then I believe you are choosing to have a closed mind condition and will remain ignorant throughout eternity, and will never know the Father of the Lord Jesus Christ. Remember Jesus said to the Pharisees they were deaf and could not hear, blind and could not see, and was completely void of any understanding, because they did not know his Father. Now what do you suppose they needed to do, so they could have their ears opened, their eyes opened, and a little substance added to their understanding?

I believe the obvious answer to that question, and to so many other simple questions, is to get to know the Father of Jesus Christ. That answer is so simple that a great mind cannot attain to the smallest end of it, like all the other questions that so many people come up with. Jesus said they were hid from the wise and prudent, not because he hid them, but because they choose to try to walk around blind. What can one do for them? How can we tell them? The Word of God is the total of what we know about the Father of the Lord Jesus Christ, or what somebody else tells us and we are taught that the word is false, and full of mistakes, and that God is not smart, or powerful enough to print a Bible that is true, not to mention speak a world into existence. That's the sum of carnal teaching.

Then where are we going to get to know the one that is the Father of the lord Jesus Christ? Maybe we can go to O'Rilley and Obama, (two of the smartest, most powerful people in the world), and the biggest outspoken critics against the Bible that I maybe ever had to listen to. They seem to know how wrong the Bible is and all about when this creation took place, where does the source of their information come from? I sure do not know.

It seems they thank they have the best source of facts available, and have proved the Bible is laughably incorrect. Maybe science is their source, scientist say we came from water running over a rock for eons of time, then evolving into this creation that we have become, sounds very likely I guess, but they cannot tell us where the rock or the water, or life came from. That causes me to start some entertainment of a little doubt, enough to not want to entrust my life and eternity to them. They don't sound all that dependable to me. Not a very good sounding foundation to me.

I'm just a simple man, and don't even claim to be looking out for all of you like Bill O'Rilley. I don't even claim to be born in kryptonite like Obama. So my opinion don't amount to much, but I am entitled to it, and believe it sounds much more convincing to me to believe God than any amount of scientist that has tried to prove God wrong for thousands of years and cannot prove one point of what the Bible says, to be false. Science changes their beliefs, opinions, and so called facts very often, several times in my lifetime alone.

I don't believe they sound like a strong enough foundation to stake the beginning of my life and my hereafter on, and feel comfortable about it. I don't believe I could sleep well, not after I have come to know Jesus and his Father, I know that I would not. Maybe their source is our schools and their college professors. Could they have told Israel their future thousands of years ago? The word of God did. Israel had schools for prophets back in the days of the judges and kings, seems that was where most of their false prophets came from, just like it is today. I believe every problem this country has today can trace their root back to our schools.

No, I would not recommend our schools for the place to get to know the Father of the Lord Jesus Christ, or any facts at all about how we were created. So where is the source of the great wisdom of the smarter than God people getting their great knowledge from? Seems like they would share a little with us instead of brags and absolute obvious lies, they call theories.

Maybe their source is the church, and then you would be forced to ask, which church? They all claim to be the right one as far as I know, and I think that would be utterly next to insane to believe that all of them can be true. So that brings us back to the Bible, which is Jesus Christ himself with no exceptions, as far as I know and I'm trying to find out more.

Anybody that cannot accept that is either deceived, subverted, willingly ignorant, or turned over to a reprobate mind. He can be that way and belong to any or every denomination in the whole world, and I would strongly recommend you to believe that fact, for God said for each of us to judge ourselves and to work diligently to make our calling and election sure, and to work out our own salvation. If you want to ignore all that and trust it to a denomination to do it for you, I sure wish you a lot of luck for you are going to need it. I've always used a smart remark I'll throw in here just for a smile, "It's a good thing I'm so smart, for if I depended on my luck, I'd be in a heck of a shape." But maybe your luck is better than mine, I hope so.

Maybe the smarter than God people's source of wisdom comes from the great carnal books they are always naming and bragging about reading or writing. I know a number of denomination that worship writers of great books. I had a very confused teenage girl, granddaughter of some of my church members, come to me with some of her problems. Her parent's family trees went in different directions and she was being torn apart between the two very different denominational teachings, which both sides were a little overboard with false teachings.

Now I know the norm here very well, on advice to me, but I was always a fan of Patrick Henry's speech about peace, and also read Jesus' saying that he did not come to bring peace, but division, but mostly because I never was very good at hiding truth to spare somebody's feelings, not even a very tender, sincere, beautiful teenage girl.

During the discussion she brought it up to me about one of her grandparent's church, saying "but we have this lady that has wrote this book of prophecies and everything she wrote has come true, just like she said," telling me that in tears. I said that is probably the biggest lie of the many they have told you, for I knew who she was talking about and had read some of her books, and considered them to be great books, but several things she prophesied did not come true and was far off the mark, and I could not rank them equal with my Bible, not to mention putting them over it.

So much for their source being from great books, I just will not buy it. I have never read one that I could believe enough to place my life on except the Bible. I've found no fault in it, and found nothing else that perfect, and it has always worked, you can depend on it. It is the one book of truth and we are told to not add or take away one thing from it, and let every man be a liar and the word of God be true. I intend to take him at his word, and found it has the power to destroy any thing that tries to ride over it. That includes Obama and all his followers. It has stood for thousands of years and still the book of knowledge, truth, wisdom, and revelations from the beginning to the end of all creation and everything in between, but almost nothing about God before he created the heaven and the earth, which is just a small thing to him. Not big enough to contain him, for he is taller than the stars which we can see for millions and millions of light years away, and he can do more than we as human beings can imagine.

Now give me a comparison to that, I would be anxious to think on it for a time. If someone knows about God before he created heaven and earth I would sure love to look into his source for that kind of knowledge.

CHAPTER 2

Names, Character, And Communication

When God sent Moses to tell Pharaoh to let his people go, Moses asked God who he was to tell them that sent him. God said to tell them "I Am" sent you. That was the most complete name he could have given for himself. It was not a cop-out, nor a dodge, nor just a nick name. What name can you put on somebody that is and has everything?

Names are very important to God, they denote character. When he puts a name on anyone or anything it goes with the character of the person or thing. There are lots of examples in the word of God. Jacob and Israel are two names given to one man and used throughout the Bible according to the character the man was operating in. When Moses asked God what his name was I can assure you that he took it very seriously, so he gave him a very serious answer, the best name there was.

If Moses should ask him, are you the creator of all things? God would say, I Am, if Moses would ask are you the giver of all knowledge and knowing ever thing? God would say, I Am, are you the one that holds all the water in the world in your hand and own the cattle of a thousand hills? He'd say "I Am," any other question the answer would be the same, he is it. I believe you would run out of questions before God would have run out of patience. Can you thank of a better descriptive name? I can't.

We try to find God inside this creation off in some corner called heaven, it is no accident that we cannot see him, it is because he is not there, he plainly says he cannot fit into it, he is too big. Don't measure the space, for God being a spirit does not need space. He can go through a brick wall and not leave a mark on it. He can dwell inside matter, and distance is nothing to him. He can see as good in the dark as He can in light, no difference with him. And these smarter than God people think they can bring him down to the level of man or beast or creeping things, measure him and judge him. If that is as smart as they are, no wonder God said he would set in heaven and laugh at us when we insist on getting ourselves into trouble, all because we want to get everything we want and have everything our way.

With seven billion people living on earth, each getting everything they want and having everything their way, I don't know much about God but I would see that as a very confusing situation. I would not want the responsibility for it under any condition or at any price. I believe I would have to put in too much overtime to please seven billion people, every one, every day.

God gave this creation to Adam and Eve, put them in charge, and told them to tend it, with food hanging off every tree. Said he would have sheltered them like a hen would have taken her little chicks under her wings and blessed them but they would not. That is about the same story all through the Bible, has not changed anywhere in it, the same old story to each of us.

Satan, through treachery and deceit, against Eve, took the garden away from them and God drove them out from the garden, told Adam he would have to work for a living, told Eve she would suffer childbirth for her sin, thinking that mankind would know better than to disobey him again, because man cannot survive and get along with one another without obeying God. Look around if you need any proof of that. With only having two boys and the whole world to live in, there was not enough room for all of them on the same earth together, so one had to be killed.

If you want to see what jealousy does to a person and how little amount it takes, look no farther than that situation. Man has a terrible hang-up, seems he never learns. I've learned a thing long ago that seems to be a hard thing for a man to conceive, if you cannot learn to be content with what you have, and then you will never be content, don't even look for it.

When men begin to reproduce on the earth, Sons of God, or angles, saw the daughters of men that they were fair, in the 6th chapter of genesis, and God was not there to guard them, moved right in took them to wife. Children were born and polluted the entire human race. God cut the life span of man down to 120 years and vowed that his spirit would not always strive with man. The rest is Bible. The best and only accurate history mankind has from then on until the end and it has come true so far just as written and the rest is very plainly in coming.

God was completely out of his creation and just appeared at divers times and various places and in various forms and very limited ways because it chose to fall apart from him. With ever chance and every opportunity they failed to make it on their own. God was left with only two choices, to take their free will away and force them to get along with him or just destroy them. But in these last days has appeared to us in the form of his son, Jesus Christ, the lamb that went back to the father in what I assume Paul referred to as the third heaven, saying he knew a man that went there. And the laws they used were not recognized in our world and apparently not comparable to anything he knew in our world, that is about all the knowledge I can find in the Bible about where God is located at. I am sure someone is saying God is everywhere. He is everywhere he wants to be. I heard the angles at the tomb tell the women that was looking for Jesus, that he could not be found among the dead. I have read several books, wrote by very intelligent men and women and not found any thing about God's dwelling out of our creation. I had to read it in the Bible, not in man's books.

We read plainly of many things God has that we do not have, and a few things we have that a spirit does not have, like male and female, reproduction ability, and their own carnal material body. God said he has withheld no good thing from us and I do not believe that he lied about anything. But we seem to have a hard time being responsible for anything he gives us.

Our world is a wonder that was created in the midst of a spiritual world that we cannot see, hear, feel, or do nothing to or with, at our own will. Carnal, (anything apart from God), cannot know nothing about it except through our minds, through which the spirit communicates it to us. We each have a measure of the spirit which is given to us by the creator, called our spirit, which God gave to each of us, of course God gave to us everything we have including time. The Spirit sees all of time, anytime it wants to, from the beginning to the end. We can only see very short flicks or pieces of a second, at a time. If we use our minds and the word of God and believe the word and spirit of God we can get big plain glimpses of time behind or in front of where we are. I believe they are called dreams and visions. God has promised us that the man that studies his word and seeks his spirit receives more of them.

A carnal mind cannot see a spirit, hear a spirit, or know anything about it. The things of the spirit are foolishness to the carnal mind. The spiritual side is the real thing not the carnal side, which is dead to God. God made man in God's image, not the other way around. I do not know anything about communication at the time or season of creation except what we get from God's word, which he gave us at a much later point in time. But it is apparent they had an obvious way of talking among themselves, God, men, and animals.

When man disobeyed God and partook of the tree of knowledge of good and evil, man died from the circle of communication and fellowship with God. I believe this is where man's mind became in two parts, the tree had two fruits, knowledge of good and knowledge of evil, God did not want us to dabble in the knowledge of evil, it is obvious that we cannot handle it.

God started another way of communication between man and

God, a long process which started with a skin for a covering and completed with a new birth into the spirit, called reconciled back to God. We can get that communication back again, but it is in the spirit not in the carnal for the carnal is evil and is dead to God and will remain dead without a mediator, he tried princes, profits, judges, kings, priest and every other way you can imagine but man would not have it. Then he sent his Son to be one of us to lead us back to the father, all of them that loved righteousness, and would become one of his children, one with his son. Jesus made plain that this spirit that him and the father would send back would be the last chance, take it or leave it, it is their last offer.

Everything on this earth is made from the same elements that this earth is made of, including man, and will remain just as dead as the earth without the spirit. God has devised a way and plan to reconcile man back to God into the spirit which is the life of anything that has life in it.

Among a lot of ways of communications he took up "writing." He started his part by writing the Ten Commandments on a stone and gave it to a chosen man called Moses. He had raised Moses out of death so to speak, (as seems to be his way of using anything or anybody) and gave him no little task, but a huge task that Moses really did not want, which is also a very usual trend with the spirit of flesh. Communication continued to be a problem. Men only wanted to speak to God through Moses but did not want to believe him, and everything they did not like they wanted to kill. They wanted to kill God's voice by trying to stone Moses and Aaron. All up through the Old Testament God tried to be their leader and caretaker. He tried every route known to reconcile man back to God, but man being so much smaller than God that the sight of facing God was so ferrous it made even Moses to fear and quake.

Man had so much pride, selfishness, jealousy, hatred, greed, and all the other fruits of the flesh till it was humiliating to man to face God. Even with God being covered with a dark cloud, man did not want to meet with God, wanted him to tell Moses and they agreed they would listen to Moses. That made humility the only way back to God and it is still the only way back till today.

The name, flesh, carries no implication of character to God and will be immediately consumed in the presents of his full glory. Jesus Christ paid the price to stand in as the mediator between man and God. It was such a great price that nobody else in heaven or earth could pay it. Not even Reverend Moon, Mohamed, or the Pope, nor something called Allah.

Peter said plainly at Pentecost, "there is no other name under heaven by which man must be saved by." People that think they can judge the character of Jesus Christ or can set in his seat and judge any other man for him, I would think they must be a little touched in the head, or lacking a little somewhere. I cannot phantom such a creature in my small mind.

I do not believe God built a Frankenstein in man, something that got too big for him to handle. I had a man tell me one time, he believed that may be what happened. No wonder God says that man is foolish

CHAPTER 3

The Two Beings In God's Creation

What God makes he makes to last forever. He creates the material and forms it into what so ever he wants to form it into and he can change it at will like the potters vessel. If he don't like what it looks like he can whoop it back up and make it into something else, including his people. It is very obvious that he don't like what flesh turned into, so he is changing it into something else. The only way is to whoop it back into the earth and make it into something else more pleasing to him, "painful, isn't it?"

God gave us a certain amount of power to do this very same thing, it's called a free will and we turned it into what it is, called carnality. I have never figured out why. My guess is it was too out match God, to set us free from the spirit that we were made from. Beginning with the Tower of Babel, building the city Babylon which stands against the city of Jerusalem till this day, and will stand against it till God destroys it completely because he didn't like the way we turned it out either.

Man is still trying to free his self from God and that way is death. Look at it from God's side, would you let man take you over and run this universe his way and God be man's servant? He has showed us time and again that if he does not intervene that there will be no flesh left, for man is destined and determined to destroy himself. Any man that thinks that he is qualified to tell God what to do and how to do it, he don't know the one God of the Israelites, and he don't know mankind either, or will not face up to truth. He doesn't know them at all. He ought to re-adjust his mind and renew it every day with the mind of Jesus Christ and do it willingly, if he wants to live past death. This seems to be everybody's dream. I don't know of anybody doing it on his own in 6000 years, except Jesus Christ. Or maybe you are one of them that believe the grave is the end. Well with you it will be. But God said what he creates he creates to last forever, just in another form. Maybe you will be a door step to one of the saint's gold mansions, at least you'll be free from the spirit of God, JOY JOY!. But Jesus says, there will be weeping and gnashing of teeth there. Have fun wherever you're at. After all isn't the world man formed having fun? Look around. It's Kind of like looking back over some of my past. I thought I was having fun but some of it, I say now, looks like a very dry fun. Of course that is hindsight.

Speaking of hindsight, what's hindsight to man is really foresight to God. You can study on that a life time. Didn't God say that the carnal side of man is contrary to God? God declared the end from the beginning. He's sitting at the end looking back at us trying to make it to him. The only way there is, is through his son Jesus Christ. Maybe you ought to be singing for him to hold your hand.

This all kind of means that when you were baptized into and with the Holy Ghost and fire you came up looking the opposite direction. And if you can't receive it and if you're walking in the same direction as you were that means you are walking the opposite direction of where you're looking. Jesus called this walking blind and in darkness and promised you will fall into a ditch or pit, both the leaders and the followers. God said to wake up out of sleep and start watching where you are walking. I know that sounds like foolishness to the carnal mind because God said it would. I'm hoping your slipping a little bit out of the carnal mind, God said it's sure death to stay there. And the mind is where the battle is. This battle is won or lost in the mind and you can be sure it is a battle and that God's people are going to win, but only God's people. Righteousness is the only thing that will dwell in God's new heaven and new earth. The word righteous means that which is up right before God. No man is righteous in himself, not one. He must wear or put on the righteousness of God's son Jesus Christ which became the seed of Abraham and paid the price for the entire world if they will just believe through their minds and don't let the god of this world blind their minds and the light of the glorious gospel cannot shine into their hearts and Jesus cannot save them. (Editor's note; sentences were made by college professors, some of the most carnal minded people on earth, maybe I should dedicate a chapter to them. I may just do that. End of editor's note)

Most writing I know much about is the forming of words out of lines by crooks, curves and length. I'm aware that there is a thing called picture writing or maybe body language but I don't think they mean much, are not very plain until somebody turns them into words of our language that we can understand. This brings up a parable form of explanation that took me many years to discern, a word spoken can only mean as much as the spirit behind it that it was spoken from and then as much as the spirit that receives it can receive it as. That is all the power and understanding it can take with it. You need to know the spirit that you are talking from and the spirit that you are talking to. That's what they meant by, what they said about Jesus when the men that was sent out to shut him up. When the men they sent out came back without him and no good news at all, the men that sent them out were very perturbed saying why haven't you brought him in, or exposed him to be the fool that he so obviously is? Has he converted you also as he has so many of the others, by the multitudes? Their reply was, no man has ever spake like this man. He speaks as one with authority.

What we are talking about is the authority of a word is the spirit that goes with it. Gods authority is with his word if spoken in Jesus' name it will accomplish what he says it will do. The confusion is in not knowing the spirit you are of. I can walk out in my yard and yell at that shade tree all day, "in the name of Jesus jump off this mountain and into the lake." I would not expect that tree to even shake. But if I walked up to it and said it from the spirit of Jesus, "jump in the lake," I would not advise you to get into its way. The difference being the spirit behind the word spoken. I'm still studying on that one. But I believe it. I'm not told I have to understand all the word of God but I'm told I better believe it to know anything about authority. Words are a mighty big subject. I suppose a person could write about them all day, and never run out of anything to write. If he thought he was running out of something to say just choose another word, and he could be gone for another day.

I've done a lot of work on this the past few years. I'd like to share a few conclusions I came up with. If I'm curious about a word I've developed the habit of grabbing my dictionary, which I try to keep handy. I found it to be helpful. The Bible says there are many voices and they are all significant. I can't help but believe it's talking mostly about words. There is no such thing as a word that is not significant, except maybe idle words and Jesus said we will answer for every idle word.

I heard a very carnally intelligent news caster and somewhat of a philosopher say that the Bible is an ideologically written book, which is true in his carnal mind. I immediately grabbed my dictionary and started a study on the word ideology. Everything I could find about it referred it as apart from reality, just something in the mind. I can see why a carnal mind and anything that is carnal is dead to God. It is apart from God. I had already took up the word carnal for a study and found a dictionary gave, completely against its character, which is to give from 3 to 20 different definitions to a simple word, it just gave one single simple definition, "Anything apart from the spirit."

I promise you that you will not find that to be so only to a very small percent of dictionary words. It's single and simple, straight to the point. Maybe you can see a little clearer what I mean by what I say "the battle is in your mind" your heart is controlled by your mind and your mind is controlled by your spirit and words only mean what the spirit behind them is and it only means what the spirit that receives it to mean. (Read it again you can get it straight)

The word authority, like every word in the Bible is a very powerful word. Seems all men are seeking for it in any form or with any means he can come up with. Among the first things that Jesus said to his disciples after the resurrection was, "I've been given all power on heaven and earth." can you wrap your mind around that much authority? I can't, my mind is too carnal but I believe it and let it go at that. Jesus certainly didn't say it with a boastful spirit but just a factual spirit. What is that to boast about? You can do nothing against the truth but for it. We communicate with words and words can only be backed up by the spirit and the authority behind them.

In my study of words, I found the dictionary to be very helpful but very scattered and broad with its meanings, as I already mention the dictionary gives 3- maybe 30 different meanings to most of the simplest of words. Then I discovered the Bible has its own built in dictionary, I call it God's dictionary. I say it don't use a word that it don't have a built in explanation even though it is hid from the wise and the prudent of carnal minds. That's why if you don't seek God, believe God, love God and study the word of God, which is the truth, the way, the light, the bread, the life and God says we are complete in him. We are nothing without him. I don't know how he could make it any plainer. We don't know God if we don't believe him (we don't get it.) get it?? If we will believe him he gives us the power to become the sons and daughters of God and joint heirs with his son Jesus Christ. Can you top that one? I've been told by Pentecostal preachers, the Bible was full of mistakes and errors. I heard that very educated, smart news castor say, "You cannot go to the Bible for truth, after all it condones slavery." Is slavery a lie? For an educated ex school teacher that puts up a new word for us to look up after almost every news cast, Mister "O" I am a very dumb man but I would like to challenge your ability to read the bible. He also says it cannot be a true book and he can prove it. He sounds like the Pharisees telling Jesus, he was casting out devils by the power of the prince of the devils. God said in that they blasphemed. I call it the same thing considering the power of words.

No wonder God said be slow to speak and be careful what we

speak, and the tongue has the power of hell fire, and he speaks from heaven, and we speak from down here on earth. I would not want to be wearing blasphemer shoes when I cross that river of Jordan.

God gave us his word which was Jesus Christ, from the beginning and was with his people in one form or another at least from the time he made Abraham the father of his children and made an everlasting covenant with him.

God says Jesus was the fire over the tabernacle at night and the smoke over it by day and lead them 40 years through the wilderness because they refused to go into the promised land, after God told them to go, that they could take the land. But they wouldn't believe him.

Jesus was the rock that Moses struck to bring forth enough water for two to five million people and their animals. More than a trickle wouldn't you think? Yes Jesus was there all along, they just couldn't see him. He's still here with us today but we still must believe him and be born into his spirit and walk in it. I didn't make that rule and know nothing I can do about it so don't get mad at me, talk to God about it. It is the twos I've been talking about from the start, the spirit and the carnal. The two sides even in our minds, and we need to know the spiritual side and know that it is the right spirit. The bible says to try the spirit, they are not all of God. Like David, pray for the right spirit.

He has promised to help you, hold you up, carry you if necessary, if you will just believe him. If you believe in God and seek him hard enough he will give you the desires of your heart. Familiar line isn't it? Well I've heard it over preached and preached wrongly many times. He did say it but he did not add to it, only if it is something that is good for you. He also said he puts into power all are leaders, he raises and lowers the nations like a drop of water from a bucket, so just blame God, right? You can if you like but I can promise you he is going to blame you right back.

He will keep his promises. Just back up and look at any situation, did not we desire the president we got? He worked feverishly to get the bottom of the pool votes; the dead weights, the minorities, the women, the young kids, and the old people. Because a fool could figure that is the vast majority of votes. All he needed to win and now he likes to remind us of it every day.

Now look at the ones that are hurting the most, lost the most, and the most deprived. It is the dead weights, the minorities, the women, the young kids, the old people that they accused the conservatives of wanting them to die and pushing them over a cliff. You see God said them that point the finger and accuse are guilty of the same thing, Romans 2nd chapter. That is so big it took me several years of study to fully see it. Then I could see everything the Democrats were doing and planning to do by what they were accusing the Republicans of, that is big, just try it yourself, others have and come back to tell me how amazed they are, at how well it works. Did God not give these people the desires of their heart? They should read also that we will reap the desires of our heart when we get it.

I ask you not to believe just me, look for your selves, across our country, back and forth, do a little math as they say, if the far left cities and states aren't going down harder, faster, first and more painful in every way. Look at California, Chicago, Detroit, and New Orleans, all the states up and around New York area just to name some of the more obvious few. If you cannot see it, then I will agree with Jesus, you are blind leading the blind and will both fall in the ditch or pit, called both by the word of God.

Look in the college dictionary at what pit means, it says a hole going down in the ground, look at God's dictionary, Jesus went down into the center of the earth, took the keys to death, hell, and the grave, from Satan and lead his souls out free. Gave gifts unto men, which was the spirit in which we can walk in him, talk in him, and he can be our father and we can be his children. Tell them college professors to put that into their test tubes and analyze it. I would like to look at that when they get it all broke down and processed. I've been told that the college professors are expected to write a book, and for certain jobs it is required. Maybe one of them can write on the truth for a change, which is the Lord Jesus Christ, and that is not a religion trying to take over our wonderful country and do away with the truth that it was built upon. It's the other way around. As I said the carnal is backwards to the spiritual way of thinking. It's an antichrist religion that is taking away our country and pretty well already done it. The Christians are acting like zombies under control of the Babylon spirit and acts like it has more power than God. Can that be possible? Yes, if the Christians will play the part of the zombies and be killed by the ones that pushes the buttons on the machine.

God has told us to stand up, not to be moved, and not back up, and to push His buttons they have more fire power than Satan, the world and the antichrist combined. I used to call the left that voted left, the zombies but I have turned that around too. Christians that play dead and will not believe and will not stand up for Jesus Christ are the zombies.

Then ask where are the Christians that will obey him and stand up in what he said? How can they stand up for what they don't believe in? How can they believe in someone they do not know? How will they know if they cannot hear or have not been told?

But they know that antichrist spirit of this world and most of them believe him, all of them that are still in the carnal and willingly ignorant of God's judgment believe him and will be burned up by the fire of Jesus Christ. He said he came back to bring fire upon all the Earth and all its works and the Heavens will be rolled up like a scroll and disappear. Where are the Christians that will be left standing till the end and will be saved because they did endure till the end? God's word said they would endure by the blood of the Lamb and the words of their testimony.

It is easy to claim to be one of those people. I desire to see a few of them but I would hardly know where to look, everyone will probably name their denomination as to where they are at. Does that mean that every denomination will have to save all its members? That doesn't sound like a very stable organization to me. God's word said there is no other foundation that can be built upon other that Jesus Christ. I believe that one will stand and God don't need two foundations for his people to build upon.

I will put it another way, if all of God's people loved, believed, and obeyed Jesus and walked in his spirit there would not be but one denomination, and the gates of hell could not prevail against it. I don't believe Christ has two bodies on this Earth, that is to say you can belong to one body and I can belong to another and we both will be all right, Do you believe that? God's word says Christ's body is not divided. Daniel said, the antichrist will take over when he has succeeded in scattering the power of the Holy Ghost. I see denominations as helping him accomplish that as much as almost anything on this earth. Sounds like a Democrat to me. It didn't take an ancient king or our democrat party to come up with the slogan, divide and conquer, it has been around since Lucifer rebelled against God and was threw out of heaven before the creation. That is just the antichrist spirit that is alive and well in the world today as it was in John's day. It is not hard to see and identify, it is under one of the two beings that God has created, he created everything to be under the spirit of Christ which is love and life, or the spirit of antichrist which has no other purpose but to kill, steel, and destroy to conquer. We each are beings of one or the other spirits, unless we are bastards, this is what God's word calls a people that denies being a child of the devil but refuses to endure the chastising of God. Again God has told us to judge ourselves. The choice is ours, and the way is clear.

Any people that is willing to destroy a whole country by dividing it with lies and hatred and tearing down its foundation that it was solely built upon just to conquer and take control of it, even when they obviously have nothing to offer it but willing to take total charge of it. The irony of it is the majority of the people do not know the spirit that they voted for, supported, and are an active part of, even when their willing to kill or destroy anything that is willing to disagree with them or get in their way in any form. The Bible is their biggest obstacle. It reviles the truth, and they are a lie. And they cannot discern the spirit that they are of?

CHAPTER 4

The Anti-Christ Is Coming

I would like to tell a very true story here that cleared something up for me and maybe someone else might be helped by it. Around something close to 40 years ago, I was saved and started seriously studying my Bible and seeking God. I was hearing a lot of "name it, claim it, grab it, stab it" "if you can believe, just pick it up and take it home with you," type of preaching. I am sure if you go to church much you know a little bit about what I am talking about.

Then I was reading in my Bible in the book of Revelations, it was obviously talking about the antichrist and stated plainly, "He would be given power over the saints and to put them to death". That about shot me out of the saddle. I was very confused and about went into a frenzy studying the word and praying and questioning God, literally giving him a hard time. Where is that power I had been hearing preached? Where is all that power I had been promised in Jesus name? Now you are telling me of a time that the antichrist is going to be given power over the saints and to put them to death. I was almost perturbed, I was thinking somebody is lying to me and I have always hated liars.

I must have prayed and fought for the answer for maybe two to three months. I accomplished a lot of growth and learned a lot of things but I wasn't finding the answer. I had about let it go, at the time my problem was about the furthest thing from my mind. I was in a church service, we were routinely called to go to the Lord in prayer, I slid off my seat and turned and knelt on my seat to start my prayer which I later referred to as my grumbling session with the Lord. I was telling the Lord what I needed and what I wanted him to do but when I started he like stopped me talking and started talking to me. I don't reckon I heard a voice but I heard him and plainly. The best I can put it into words is, "Yes, you read it in my word and it is right, nothing wrong with it. I put it there, but there is something else I want you to know. I am not the one that is giving him the power." He then rolled something before my eyes the best I can describe it, was like a television screen rolling over. I don't know what I saw, I cannot describe it, but I fully knew what it was. It was God's church world and it was about the filthiest thing I had ever looked at, I got the message.

About that time the rest of the people were finishing their prayers and setting up. I got up turned and sit down. I think I must have been half in shock, saying to myself over and over "No wonder Jesus wept." Look at the church if that is the only light that the world has to walk by, no wonder it is walking out into a cyst pool. Where are the kings, profits, pastors, that he has sent?

We have killed, stoned, and beheaded some of them and rejected the others, where are the Christians? You might remember that the church started our schools, and our schools started our government and drew up our constitution saying the government has no power over the church and could not pass a law or hinder a religious institution. The only thing they consider a religion is something off of the Holy Bible. Our president will not use the word holy with Bible but uses it with the Koran every time. Are they the same thing? Is Allah and God the same person? I've been told they are the same thing by bishops, news castors, cardinals, and Holy Ghost filled preachers in our own ranks.

Is Christ divided? Will the people called by his name make it? If they don't, God will have to resurrect his undercover Christians, I hope he has some. My prayer is I hope he will uncover them. I believe it is about time, we need help, Help!!!

The church that is supposed to be the light of the world needs a light for its self because it doesn't need to lead that antichrist into Hell. That is already a sure thing on its own without the Christians leading it from the front. Don't that mean they will go in first? I wonder... from where I am looking at it, I have very little hope for them after death.

In the parable of the seed sower, God is the sower, the seed is the word, but if it falls upon a rock, or too hard of ground, it is worth nothing and the fowls of the air devoir it. If it falls in briers and bushes it is chocked out, but if it falls into the earth and dies it can sprout and make a stalk with ears of many grains of corn.

Where are the workers to prepare the fields and gather the harvest that is going on every day? I am afraid too many people are too busy trampling the Earth and the sprouts to help the stalks to produce. These are workers of iniquity and God will cut these asunder with the wicked. They are tending wild seeds in God's garden which he prepared and sowed with good seed. Where is the Christians that are tending his garden? It is surely not the schools or families that is feeding our kids and maturing young children. It's not our law makers they have threw the seed out of the home, schools, courts, the national parks, the military, the whole country, and shame and make fun of anybody that will dare mention his name. Our president said to the world "This is not a Christian nation." It's not a nation of liberty anymore either.

You don't dare ask a government official what you cannot do on your own property, if he answered you it would be thousands of pages of paper. It would be a book so big you could not carry it out. If you ask him the things you could do on your own property that he would have no authority to come and check and ask you about, I believe you would go away with a blank piece of paper.

Where are the people that will stand up and even believe that the Bible is true and is God's word? Several years ago some outfit took a survey and claimed by their own confessions that the entire television programmers were 82% atheist and had no use for God in what they were doing and living. I seriously believe that it has not improved very much since. God says he will turn into hell any nation and any people that would dare do that. They wonder and cannot see what is wrong with this country. Why can't they open their eyes? Why don't they ask a man of God? God said too. Instead they hate anything even called righteous.

Jesus is the only man to walk on this Earth that was righteous, and then any man that has any righteousness, it belongs to Jesus. We are just wearing Jesus for our righteousness and it's supposed to cover our self and all flesh.

I established most of my principles in my early formative years. As Paul said in God's word it is not profitable for me to glory anyway or anytime at all but we get tempted and talk like a fool every once in a while. I am not any smarter than anybody else but I have always felt I was just as good as anybody else. I come to believe I have lived 74 years in an indestructible body because I can about match most of anybody else in experiences and miles and rough times and dangers, and Satan has not destroyed me yet, even though he has tried almost every way he can come up with.

Just lately more than every God has showed and told me how big a hand he had in leading and training and protecting me in everywhere I have been. But I was up in my thirties when I turned my life over to him. I saw almost immediately that he could run my life better than I ever did. I have slept better ever since. I am a complete new man, as we all say, I am not perfect but in God's eyes I am for I wear his righteousness and God has said the carnal mind cannot see that, don't know that, cannot have that, and above all he cannot understand that. What I was into before I was in this life and alive to the world, and in another life I was far from just wasting my time, for God was in control without me knowing it. I reckon I dabbled around in about every sin known to man and God. I used to say I been over half the world and saw an Arkansas goat roping, that, I thought covered a bunch. I am not proud of much of it but I learned a lot of lessons and carry a few scares.

I tell that I am going to walk into Heaven someday looking around and see an angel setting over a ways looking like he has just about been had, beat down, used just terribly. Somebody is saying to him "What happened to you?", he replies "Oh they assigned me to watch over that Bill Wilson through his time down there on Earth."

Speaking of time and times is a very interesting word. God doesn't see time as we do, of course he doesn't see anything as we do. If we want to see things correctly we have to turn it around and see it backwards to the way of men. You can work on that for a lifetime. I am 74 and still looking and learning every day.

Time is just something we can measure by something else. Did you ever see a date in time that God set? We figured dates out for ourselves. We started using the birth or death of Jesus for a marker. The world now using that for a marker but would have been confusing for them to have tried to use Christ birth before he was born. God could have if he wanted to. Of course we would not have understood anything about it. Time sets before God, all of it, he can look at it all or any part anytime he wants, from the beginning to the end. Only he knows when the end is coming on us, but right now we are setting in 2013 the year of our Lord.

We don't know about the future unless we read the Bible and the spirit reveals it to us. We don't know anything about life before our time but we see marks left and what somebody tells us. Our God is the surest thing that is in this universe. I don't see how a person can be born and open his eyes and look around and not know there is a God. Every record we have tells us in every known time, man has worshipped something. Usually things he could not control, that is why people who don't know the real God has himself many Gods. Usually something he thinks is helping him and can give him what he wants.

You see somebody worshipping a god he can use, he is worshipping a false god. The God of the Bible is using man not man using him. It's like I am always saying man gets everything backwards to God, if he can't get looking the other direction he will never see where he is going.

God has told us much more about end times than he has about the time of the beginning. Maybe it's more important. If you look at man he is working feverishly to establish his beginning, wait, hasn't that already been very well established? God's word said to "Not look to things you see but look to things you cannot see". If you are seeing spiritual that will not sound confusing at all to you, but if you are seeing carnally you can forget it, you'll not get it.

Remember when they were talking about sending a missile, or something anyway, to Pluto hoping it would send back information to help explain our beginning. I ask, reckon their expecting to find a note hanging out from under a rock starting out with--In the beginning....

I guess I am thinking foolishly or is it them? I don't know but I am sure God knows. He knows all about sending moving pictures over the world and catching them on the other side of the world on a flat screen. And he knew about instant replay long before baseball figured it out, and knew about recording long before Hank Williams and Frank Sinatra made big on it. Now can you imagine what he still has in store that he hasn't revealed unto us yet? He says we can't, and I believe him.

What power the spirit world has, and man is so curious and determined to move in on it, but has nothing more than a glimpse of it while we are in this fallen condition, for God's glory would consume us in an instant in his full presence. His son volunteered to pay the fleshly sacrifice to save us, not our flesh, it must die, for the end of all flesh is clearly predestinated.

But our soul and spirit can be saved and dwell in the spirit world with him forever if we fully believe him and endure this fleshly body till the end, through his son Jesus Christ. Not through any other man's organization or any people or nation's religion, but through Jesus Christ the only one that will be at the judgment to see if he knows us or not.

No denomination or any country's religion died for you, just Jesus. No wonder so few are going to make it. It's a straight and narrow way you can get off on the right or left, or back slide, or quit or any other way, it's your choice.

The parents of the children have the responsibility for the children and will be held responsible. God says they are excuseless o'man. Them that find their life here on Earth will be burned up with the earth. This all sounds a little scary to me so as for me I think I will choose to walk in the spirit with God and forsake this life and to look for his coming back to get me, and I'll give my signature to approve this message.

God sent Moses to lead his people out of Egypt. They were following very reluctantly, and when they needed water and was threatening to stone Moses and wanting to go back to Egypt, which is a type of sin and of the world that God was trying to lead them out of so he could be their God and he could take care of them, of course man has to be proven too minute by minute and God wanted them to love and fellowship with and trust him and even be his children so if you are having trouble with your youngsters you might read your Bible and see Gods problem and give you some understanding.

He destroyed the world that was and started over again and offered to do it again for Moses' sake and start over again with Moses. But Moses stood in the gap for them and would not let God destroy them, just like Jesus stood in the gap for the whole world later on. God said he would not destroy them just yet but would lead them that are 20 years old and upward and saw his miracles, around in the wilderness for 40 years until that generation died off then he would lead their children into the promise land. God's super table will be full.

I've heard a lot of arguing and opinions on how long a generation is, well that generation was forty years but man's dictionary says that a generation is "that being generated" that told me along with my Bible dictionary that the length of a generation is variable, end of argument.

CHAPTER 5

We Are To Follow God, Not Lead Him

When they rebelled so vigorously over running out of water and complained about the food, wanted to stone Moses and go back into Egypt, God told Moses the first time to strike the rock and bring them forth water. The first time he did. But this second time God told Moses to speak to the rock, which was Jesus, but Moses in anger running out of patience went before the rock and started, what I call an I sermon, Saying must I strike this rock again, you rebels, and I bring you forth water. God said, Moses you put yourself in front of me, and you will not go into the promise land with them, for that self-spirit is what I am trying to get out of them, meaning we crucified Christ once, you except that and don't strike him again, you speak to him and if you are born again and in his spirit he will hear you and you will hear him.

So Moses did not go into the promise land, and in giving his law he said if a kid which cannot be handled take him before the congregation and stone him to death. Meaning a child must be taught to follow, not lead. Remember when our president talked about going by the Bible to raise kids, he said guess he could go to the book of

Exodus and kill them, like our God said. Maybe I could send him a copy of my book, like Chavez, I believe was close to his name, gave him. But I doubt if carnal minded, God hating, Obama every read it even though it was from one of his brothers and I am sure he would not want to read mine.

God was working hard to show a precedent he was going to keep. The only way to righteousness was through Abraham who he had made a father to all them that would believe and obey, like Abraham. They would be called the children of Abraham and the carnal blood line had nothing to do with being Abraham's children but a spiritual blood line consisting of the blood of several million animals till Jesus came alone and gave the perfect sacrifice, once and no more.

The confusion of who are the children of Abraham has shed more human blood than all of the animal's blood all up through the Old Testament. You animal lovers might thank Jesus for saving more animals than all of your organizations could ever save. I know a number of people that still give animal sacrifices till today, some of them to the devil. So many lessons to be learned here, one of them is if a child cannot come to obedience he is dead while he is living.

God killed all of the Earth except 8 souls, and an ark full of beast. He slew thousands at a time, many other times since. God has sworn by his own name that he gets no pleasure in slaying the wicked. That don't mean he won't do it. In the New Testament times he slew a man and his wife for lying to the Holy Ghost. God is the biggest killer of mankind on the pages of history. Do you feel qualified to put him on trial? Job thought he could till he meet and saw him and was put on the witness stand himself. God asked him probably a few hundred questions. Job could hardly answer a one of them.

It kind of sums up to this, God is the judge and it is pretty difficult to judge the judge in any court or case. In God's court if you're pleasing self, (A dead hunk of meat, to God), then you're not pleasing God. So invariably you do not choose to please God, but self, and that is the wrong direction to be looking. God says look above to things not seen not things on Earth that you can see.

Hope is to look for something you don't have, why would you

hope for something you already have? God says by faith and hope we walk, not by sight. God is judging every day and we are receiving the end of our faith.

We have tendencies to make and receive problems for ourselves that sometimes don't even belong to us. There is no problems that are not common to man no matter how much we think we are the only one that has these problems, or this many problems, that's just not so. God says there are angels encamped around anybody that fears him, Problems are only as big as we make them out to be and we are not judged by our action as much as our reaction. Most of the time a problem is not a problem until we react to it, usually the best way is to ignore it, but sometimes you can't maybe. To handle a problem, varying on the nature of the problem after all the explaining I have decided we are not going to be judged by the problem but how we handle the problem. I reckon that is what life is made up of and Jesus says we are already judged by the word of God and we can judge ourselves by it and he will not have to judge us. We must do that by the word of God only. We just need to put our full trust in him, hard for us to do.

That is why when we threw out the word of God we have threw out God. God said he will turn into Hell any nation or any people that will dare do that, (Psalms 9). I have been pondering on the difference between the flesh and the spirit and the more I study the more I feel like I am not out of my mind, just out of my carnal mind. I have said some tremendous things since I have been writing this, maybe without half understanding what I said. Let me recover a few of them.

When I said the battle between the spirit and the flesh is in the mind let me reemphasize a little, you hear people talk about an out of the body experience. Where did they go? I don't believe there is any other world known to man but the spirit world and the carnal world I have come to many visions and revelations the past few months I have questioned my own sanity. Ponder a few of them with me. The only communication with the spirit world we have is in the word of God or by dreams and visions, and revelations. I really don't know of any other, it seems all of the dreams and visions have all been out of the body experiences, this leaves the word of God and revelations. The word of God is not in my body except in my mind. Isn't it about so with the other three also? Then why does the body or man or flesh want to be apart from the spirit of God which is the only life the body has in it and when it leaves the body the body is dead, the only thing left is the soul, it goes out of the body now for it has no use in staying in a pile of dirt that it cannot control or even keep together anymore. Where does it go? Jesus' spirit was going into his Father's hands.

Man's, is apart from God as the body chose to be, and is with the spirit that was threw out of Heaven by Michael and the boys, after losing the war in Heaven. If their independence is so pleasing why do they seek so hard to occupy a fleshly body and to control it to death knowing that apart from God is sure death for it? I guess it knows that there will be many more bodies coming along preferably offspring from the body it just killed for it is more familiar to him because he is apart from God and is defeated and powerless and needs a vehicle to ride, powered by God. But God is not going to always strive with man because man chose death back in the garden and has to be reconciled back to God through Jesus Christ and rebirthed back to God and proven before he can live eternally with God, apart from all flesh, for all flesh has come to an end with God. Self must die to accomplish that.

Wake up the spirit of God in you before it is too late. God's word referred to the flesh as a body of death. I seem to ponder on this so much to understand it, seems I have about come to the point to despise my own flesh, maybe all flesh, it is so unclean and some people are so proud of it. I don't understand. No wonder God said he hated a proud look. I have been preaching and praying to see things from God's position, because if we don't we don't see it correctly. God said to study the scripture they are what tells you of me. I know a lot of people that call themselves Christians that do not believe in a born again experience. One told me they believed one birth is enough. God said that Adam and Eve died and all that are born of them are born into a body of death and if you are not born into the spirit you will remain dead and will not see the kingdom of God and have no life in you. And they think they can talk at the father and have peace, joy, contentment, and satisfaction. Look around and see how many people do you see that do that and convincingly have these things? Maybe they are trying to convince themselves. Very few stand out from the world and goodness knows the world don't have it. No wonder Jesus said if you find your life here you're going to lose it when you get to the next crossing. Why would they think that one birth is enough when God's word says it isn't?

The only answer is they do not believe the word of God. I've even been told by a number of them that they don't. One said to me we believe parts of the Bible. How can they do that except to be able to choose what part they want to believe? How sound is that? How much of my salvation do I want to put on a foundation of what somebody else chooses to believe? Let me answer that if I may, not one thread of it, thank you just the same, but I believe the word of God.

I am sure you're thinking, how do you know the Bible is the word of God? I can answer that with a few hundred answers, it's proved that a few million times since time began, it has never failed, it works always, has never let me down, time has not put one dent in it. There is not a subject it does not cover, and it is hid from the wise and the prudent of the carnal mind, but revealed to babes, sucklings, and fools of the world.

Do you need to hear a few more reasons? Well here they are, it's the only truth there is, God said let all men be liars and the word of God be true. Jesus Christ is the word and the word is Jesus Christ. He is the way, truth, light, and the life. He is everything. IS that good enough reason? I'll warn you of another thing, anyone trying to wrest the scriptures to their own understanding will do so to their own destruction. You can read that in the book of Peter.

Another question I've been trying to answer is, how can these spirits apart from God captivate a body so completely it can make a body take a gun and put it to their head and pull the trigger or to someone else's head? I suppose there must be many ways. I believe all of them must be through the mind, the battle ground between the spirit and the flesh. I am sure that mind altering drugs must be one of the biggest contributors to suicide. They have become more numerous around my community the last few years, two of them within a week close enough to me to be called my neighbors. All you can really do is wonder why and how?

Jesus said you cannot spoil a vessel of goods unless you first bind the strong man of it. Who is the strong man of your mind? The word of God says Satan can blind your mind until the glorious light of the gospel cannot shine into your heart and Jesus cannot save you, might that be the way to bind the strong man?

I mentioned the mind being the battle ground between the spirit and flesh, I have about come to despise my own flesh it is so contrary to the spirit. I knew I sort of wrote myself into a small corner at the time. Well I have slept a night and day on it, guess what, more dreams, more visions, and more revelations, Let me see if I can come up with more words. I am convinced that God despises our flesh also. Let me give you some of the word of God.

What did the lepers have to yell out 2 times at anyone approaching them? Unclean, Unclean, for it was a plague of uncleanness and the leper was to dwell outside of the village until he was healed. How many times did God slap leprosy on one of his own people to convince them to obey him, even Moses, anything that was consecrated to the Lord was considered holy but if it was touched by flesh that was not sanctified then the thing touched was considered defiled and unholy.

Count the flesh God has destroyed and committed to completely destroy it all off of the Earth along with the Earth it has touched. Doesn't that conclude God despises your flesh? So why should I feel guilty? After all God has demanded the flesh be dead and baptized into the name of Christ before we approach him. Paul says then are we not all dead? God says no flesh will ever glory in his presence. When I see and hear flesh glorying I have concluded God's presence is not there. For God did not lie, so he might be about to slay that person, I will be afraid for that person and am praying for him.

The only way you can get away with glorying in the flesh is to set yourself apart from God. I don't want to go there, for I don't want to ever put myself in front of God in any form at all. Look at what he did to Moses and Nebuchadnezzar and Herod or anyone else that thought they could set themselves in the seat of God. That is the very spirit of the antichrist in progressive form when he thinks he has attained the seat of Christ he starts claiming he is God. That's why God is going to put into the hearts of them 10 end time kingdoms to burn Rome off of the map is when the antichrist figures out God is supposed to set up in Jerusalem instead of Rome. Study it in Daniel and Revelations.

I hear preachers and book writers saying the United States is going to be that antichrist kingdom, seems that they cannot read our Bible without fabricating it to fit the Muslims teachings that has us being the great Satan, Lord help them. It is blind people like them that is trying to take us there, they do have us tore down very low I will have to admit. But not that low.

The 10 kingdoms that God talks so much about in his word is the feet and toes hanging off the bottom of the Roman kingdom that was never defeated but went into perdition and split down into 2 kingdoms called the East and the West. The power and the wealth of the world is going back to the east leg like God said it would, as everything that has broken off from God has went east since Cain went east from the known world of that time, Lot choose to go east from Abraham and ended up in Sodom. Didn't the cowboy always ride off into the sunset after he settled the towns? God's word has always moved west, now we are the west, but we will lose our dominion back to the east but it's not God giving them that power and wealth but God's church, as I have already wrote about. America has stopped the antichrist in his tracks at least two times, but after one of the very best of our presidents, Truman, turned us into limited warfare during the Korean War, I said then, we would never win another major war again. What did God tell Israel after Joshua and Saul would not completely destroy the countries about them to take the land that God told them to and to kill everything in it that breathed? He finally got tired telling them too, so he told them now I won't let you destroy them, I'll leave them right beside you for a thorn in your flesh and every time you won't hear me I'll turn them loose on you until you do, hasn't that been the way it's been? And he is going to gather every nation against Israel until they say blessed is he that cometh in the name of the Lord. God does not bless limited warfare, never has, and I don't assume he ever will.

Israel is the fig tree that we are told to watch for his coming. Read your Bible, Ok? I don't think we are going to have to wait much longer. I am the one that has preached 30 to 40 years that I can see at least 10 years before his coming and believe I can see 40 or 50 years, while I hear preachers jump up and down about a rapture that could come tomorrow. They should read Thessalonians just for a start. I have started drawing back my predicted time a little and believe we are not promised a lot more time now but I am certainly not preaching a rapture yet. I don't believe I have words to describe how foolish and contrary to scripture that is, in the way they try to preach it.

God says not to be shaken by that kind of teaching, that Christ is maybe coming tomorrow, for he is not coming till that man of sin be revealed and goes on to explain who he is talking about. I detest people who wrest one scripture to call another scripture a lie. I am sure there is something badly wrong with that kind of Bible studying and teaching.

CHAPTER 6

God's Worst Enemies Among His People

God's word talks of vain jangling and not understanding the things they say nor where of they affirm, and let that kind of people be accursed. We are told to just leave them alone. But it's hard to do when you love them and know their problem, but I have learned as long as their minds are blinded and they refuse to hear there is not much you can do but pray for them and turn them over to Satan that they might learn.

Speaking of learning, where do we send our kids for learning? To schools of all kinds of names, shapes, sizes, and purposes and what do they work with? Our children's minds. I call our colleges, brain washing institutions. Under president Carter the National Education advisor, head of their union, said when they send their kids to us, they are sick in their little minds with such things as a fear of God and Hell and such foolish things. We have to unprogram their little minds so they can reach their full potential in learning. Carter was elected under waving a born again Christian flag, he gave that union a cabinet member level job in his administration of course promising them that, was one of the big deciding factors in getting him elected. She was also one of the first ones Reagan kicked out of the White House when he took office. I was ask once what did Reagan do that was so great, well there's one thing. Where are the Christians? I'm not just a little bit confused I am about totally. Where are the churches, where are the preachers? I believe they went to that union run college.

You are not allowed to pastor a church of any size without a wall full of Egyptian plaques. I am not saying that out of any envy or jealousy for I cannot think of a job I would dread any more than pasturing one of them college run churches. When it comes to education there is nothing I can think of that is any more talked about than education unless it would be the weather and you cannot fix either one by throwing money at it.

You'll never improve education until you improve what they teach. They need to at least mix in a little bit of truth and get the government completely out of it. Every time a politician talks he is talking of lies and messing with our minds, the battle ground between the soul and spirit. We need to get our minds right. God's people have already lost their freedom, and our country is going over the cliff. One of the Muslims said a while back they were going to fly their flag over our capital. I said all they have left to do is raise their pole. We already have one running the White House, and the country, end running the Congress and the Supreme Court over our constitution. Disowning and blaspheming the Bible. When are we ever going to wake up? The Bible says it is high time. If it wasn't so serious and pitiful I could almost laugh at the commercials of how the Jews are persecuted, poor, and need food, and money, money. What people is there that don't need food and money? What the Jews need is Christ, did not God tell them that he would take care of all their needs and proved it 40 years in the wilderness. Oh, I forgot they don't believe the Bible, right? So what is the use in telling them and especially when we don't believe it either and following their footprints down the same road? God said he would set in Heaven and laugh when their calamity comes upon them, and turn any people or nation into Hell that would not remember him, Jews first. The Bible is no help when you don't believe it. That is about the bases of New Testament teaching. So once again, where are the believers and what do they believe?

The government has outlawed our Bible while it has required the Koran to be taught in our so called public schools, another name that is a lie, they are government schools. How much say so does the public have in the schools today? How much control do you have over what your schools are teaching?

Notice how the government is so good at choosing beautiful names for anything they come up with. I think politicians major in college in that subject.

So I conclude that our God hating, government run schools, from college professors down to kindergarten, turning out false profits, false teachers, lawyers, politicians and professional liars are certainly the worst enemies among God's people in this country. They are going to be directly responsible for the downfall of the greatest nation that has ever been on the face of this earth. It is defiantly going down. God said our life would be spared but our dominion would be gone. I think that has just about happened.

CHAPTER 7

—◇◇◇—

Give God Glory In Everything

All of the money we spend belongs to God, every penny of it and he says we are stewards of it, and will be held accountable to him. We spend it now in trillions in this country and don't give God one ounce of glory for it. How much longer do you think he is going to keep on blessing and allowing that? Look at it, does the future look prosperous to you? God has said so many times, "consider your ways." the truth is we give, as a people, so little consideration to anybody besides ourselves that consideration is about as scarious as hen's teeth and none at all to God. Reckon how he feels about that?

After studying the Bible, history, the world condition, I don't believe a one of them ten end time kingdoms will be a kingdom of the west leg of the Roman Empire. But will be of the east leg of the Old Roman Empire consisting of the Middle East countries that are in such turmoil today. God has said they will rise up and the wealth and power of the world will be given back to them after the west has put God's people, the Jews, back into their land.

The great Whore of the book of Revelations, not a beast but a beast rider, is defiantly of the west leg and will be burned up by the ten kingdoms. It is named plainly as a city that has influenced every nation and every religion in the world. That shouldn't be too hard for an 8 year old to figure out but our teachers, lawyers, and politicians have no clue. So we are sending our money and power back to the east as fast as we can, just as God said we would, not that it pleases him but he just knew we would. He knows all things.

It is the dream and plan for the east to kill Christians and Jews and rule the world and the God that created it. They now know if they can unite the east against true religion they can do it. We seem to be doing all we can to help them. It's our choice because we are becoming a country of God haters and blame him for everything we do, just like he said we would do, just as it says in the book of Revelations. Do we expect him to stop us? We will only know God if we choose too, and that in our spiritual minds not our carnal minds.

I have talked about the battle being over such things as control, money, peace, communications, and so many other things all of them being expressed around or with words, each word being a rabbit trail. I'll try to come back to one already started instead of starting a new one.

This creation is divided by twos as is most everything that God created. He made a left he made a right, he made an up he made a down, he made a north he made a south and on and on. He made a carnal (anything apart from the spirit) he made a spiritual, they are contrary one to the other, we are born into the carnal first and God wants us to be rebirthed into the spirit but there are a few simple requirements and God is the only one that can do it for us.

The first thing we better hear is there is nothing carnal going to be accepted, not even a carnal mind. The mind is the meeting place for the battle, the carnal mind against the spiritual mind, we must choose sides. The Word of God is the only spiritual side and by far is going to be the winner. God has already won the battle for us and declared the winners and losers and named the rewards for both sides. Study your Bible and read all about it, if you would just believe him you will get your mind right and choose his side and wear his yoke, and pick up his cross and follow him. He promised it would be easy and his burdens light, but the way of a transgressor is hard.

As he told Paul it's hard to kick against the pricks, so get your minds right. As we have said "The Bible is the word of God." The word of God is Jesus Christ given to us by God the father who gave us the world and everything in it. Set it apart from himself and blessed it and thought it was beautiful and perfect, but he had no one to tend it that was of it.

Some of our very best teachers and writers that have devoted some of the most labor and time to the studying and teaching it as any man I know of,(May God bless them and I thank God for them), but they teach a preadamite world and that Lucifer was in charge of it and failed. I don't see that the Bible teaches that, but I believe the bible does teach that Lucifer is in charge of the creation now and is for sure going to fail and fall. So I don't know anything about a world before this world and cannot affirm it either way, but I do know the word itself and the spirit which is the same thing is all I have beside what somebody else tells me.

You know what wise men of the world say, believe only half of what you see and none of what you hear, (That's what they say). I am not real sure about how true that is but I can assure you I lean pretty hard in that direction and would advise anyone to do the same thing and work out their own salvation. I can give you many scriptures to back that up but would prefer you study it yourself.

Have you ever heard it said "God made everything in twos"? Well I have, a very long time ago, and now you have heard it. It is very true. For we are living in two different worlds, ever hear the old country song, "We Live in Two Different Worlds, Dear? I think maybe Eddie Arnold might have sung it. We live in a world that is in a world. Each one has its own god. Jesus said no servant can serve two masters, he will choose one or the other, hate the one and love the other, or hold to one and despise the other. These two worlds have their masters, heads, or gods, call them what you may. You cannot serve both. We each have to choose.

The best I can describe these worlds, one is of flesh and fallen man, and the other is the spiritual world of God. God has cleaned up his world and threw Satan out of Heaven and he landed down here on Earth with 1/3 of God's angels referred to as stars. Now God is in the process of finishing the cleaning up job on Satan which will have to include burning up the entire Earth with everything on it but will not do it until he has saved every soul on it with and by his spirit that will accept his spirit.

That means everything concerning flesh and everything which is apart from God will be burned up and off them, through the fire that was brought back by Jesus Christ before they can be saved. If we find our lives here we will lose it at judgment, Jesus has plainly said this, if we don't believe Jesus Christ we are not the least bit concerned are we? So we will choose this doomed world and worship the antichrist and hate the real Christ, read the Bible, tells you all about it. You will spend eternity with your choice.

That is a long time to say the very least, without God that gave you light and life to start with, he has warned us each and every one, you might give it some thought, sounds like a bargain to me but if you cannot hate the worldly side, it's a rough decision, I'll assure you.

Don't blame God he is allowing it to be as rough on us as he can tolerate himself especially if you fear him, and have a broken up spirit on this Earth, and dissatisfied with this Earth. He died to save you. If you are full of pleasure and pride on this Earth he hates you but will let you enjoy it if you don't get in his way of performing his word, for it's the only Heaven you will ever see.

Don't worry so much about them that have committed suicide, it don't guarantee them heaven but it don't guarantee you a right to send them to hell either. I'd say they have a much better chance of Heaven than any of them that is ready to send them to Hell. Aren't you glad that only God has the last word in the final judgment? I sure am.

He says he has paid the price for our salvation and made it so easy to accept that we are without an excuse if we don't accept his plan. The only reason he can see for not accepting it is we do not believe and trust him and we love this present world more than the world that he has prepared for us.

Look at it this way, if God takes any part of this world to the new Heaven or new Earth it will be polluted, unclean and no better than the old one that he just destroyed. So he will destroy it completely, as God didn't destroy it completely in the days of Noah but saved eight souls and an ark full of animals. I don't believe God saved every species of animals on the Earth, just the ones that obeyed him and went to Noah and got on the ark for him. Smart men don't have a clue as to what happened to all them dragons and dinosaurs and such prehistoric animals.

Then if you read your Bible, there is no such thing as prehistoric anything in our world, even time. Try telling that to a college professor you will learn you cannot tell a man anything that thinks he is smarter than God. I would bet many of you are thinking of me right now, well he sure thinks he is smart. No, I am a very thick and hard headed dummy, but let me remind you I have a spirit dwelling in me that knows everything, even the deep things of God and he is defiantly smarter than any college professor.

I believe it was Will Rodgers that said there was nothing dumber than an educated man out of the field that he was educated in. Of course Will Rodgers would not be considered a very smart man in today's time even though he was asked to run for president by both parties in his time. We come a long way, baby.

Communication must have started in the Garden of Eden, about all we can know is they used it, for we have record of it in the Bible. I believe we can assume it was a spiritual form, maybe what we call telepathic or something of that form. I am talking of Adam, Eve, snake, and God. We know that God walked with Adam in the cool of the day, that might have been morning or evening, we can assume they had communication for he called to them in the garden when they thought they were hiding. They answered but we don't know in what form.

God said Able's blood was calling to him from the ground after Cain had slue him but we don't know in what form it all was done. Paul wrote in God's word that Able is testifying to us until today, but didn't say in what form. Can you imagine how big our Bible would be if God would have covered all them rabbit trails of details with writing in the word of God? We could have spent a life time of the time God give us and not had enough time to have read it all, and it would not have been any help to us if we would not have believed it and had not the capability to attain that much knowledge. God giving it to us would have made it a waste of time. Can't you see what a waste of time it is to try and prove that God is a liar and we are smarter than God when we know so little to start with?

We don't even know how to communicate with God in the carnal, not to mention the fact we know so little about communicating heart to heart with one another and most of the time we can't do it, and when we can we find there is almost nothing two of us can agree on or come together on for we all have our own heart, body, spirit, soul, and there is only one common denominator and that is God.

He is one with his son Jesus by the spirit of God, and even though we cannot understand we have an invitation to be born into it but carnal and flesh cannot be taken there, mostly because there is no communication to be had there, for God is the head of his spirit, which is the head of his church and his son Jesus which is its head.

All the head the world has is on and under the heads of the Babylonian beast seen by Daniel and John in the books of Daniel and Revelations that John wrote to the churches of Asia. Read your Bible as I am always saying, if you want to know what has happened, read your Bible, if you want to know what is happening, read your Bible, if you want to know what is going to happen, read your Bible. If you cannot believe the Bible then just believe O'Rilley and Goldburg and the other false profits. The world is full of them you can choose the one you like, just about any of them thinks that God is a liar and each of them know more than God even though there is hardly two of them that agree together and they change their mind every few years consistently. How stable is that?

I've not seen any changes in scripture all up through the years we have had them. We have had some of them for thousands of years. People say they have changed it all up through time, show me one change, don't tell me about it. I would like to see what Bible the people had 4 billion years ago that Goldburg tells us about, the years not the Bible for I don't believe he can produce the Bible or the years, lots of luck trying.

In all the new technology and smart kids that can talk all over the world all at once all the time, I'll bet not one of them can call up God and have a conversation with him. I have never heard of that piece of technology. I have been expecting something like that, the devil's empts would be glad to talk to anybody on any phone if God would allow them to. Just another way of knowing God is still in control.

Sons of God before the flood took women for wives and had children and polluted the human race and grew giants on the Earth. One of the reasons God had to destroy the Earth that then was in Noah's time. The infection picked back up after the flood but God is going to see that it don't happen the next time. The next destruction will be with the purifying fire of God and nothing touched by anything unclean will survive it. God don't see touched as the exact same way we see it but the effect is the same.

The word was a way God chose to communicate to man. He gave us many facts and commands in the word about the word. He taught us how to write and understand words then gave us his word to study about him. He told us to not add any words to his word and not to slant or pervert his word in any way or form. Not for the sick, poor, rich, handicapped, nor the deprived. The main purpose I am trying to accomplish by my preaching and this writing is to stir up, all interest I can in somebody, to read and study the Word of God like Jesus told us over and over so many times to do. If they don't get an interest or hunger for it, it will do very little for them to read it. They will probably get more from reading Alleyoop or Peanuts, if they can't believe the word. I learned early if I can't sell people on the word, they cannot hear and nobody can help them.

I knew a man, several years back, that I learned I could pretty well depend on to come by my house at least once a month, usually when he got his check and had purchased his alcohol and built up his courage. I had just started preaching a little and had come out of a pretty rough crowd that would make his crowd look like school children, and I reckon the Devil would send him by to temp me and tare me down but it built me up instead, kept me studying the Bible, after around two years I finally got called by him to take some brothers with me to the hospital and held a little baptism service at his bed side.

Long story there, but anyway at one time he brought in his blood brother with him, they came in and he introduced me to his brother by saying, "Now here is a man that can save you," I appreciated the compliment but felt I needed to set the record straight at once.

I said, no I could not save a fly if you brought one to me, but I know a man that could save him, of course I was talking about Jesus and it gave me a starting place. The Bible teaches the engrafted word is able to save your soul, it also teaches the ones that have the spirit of God belongs to him and the ones that don't have it is none of his and says it's not difficult to tell them apart. The ones that are of the spirit will be minding the things of the spirit. The ones that are of the flesh will be minding the things of the flesh. How hard is that to see?

Now back to these people writing and teaching that I studied about, usually refers to the United States of America as the greatest country there ever was. Which may be so, I wouldn't know how to judge that, but they act like the Bible is wrote from America out, in that they are wrong. To start with America was not in existence when the Bible was written, it was written from Jerusalem, God's city, out to the world, and ends in the same place. America has a small part to play in any part of the Bible. Writers try so hard to make America, especially in these end times, play the biggest part in God's plan, even to being the Great Satan or the antichrist itself. America isn't even the great whore of Revelation. I believe God was talking as much directly to America in Isaiah when he was defiantly talking about the west kingdoms of this world that was formed out of the west leg of the Roman Empire, or the sixth head on the Babylonian beast of Revelations. When he said, it's just a small thing that I blessed you and raised you up to set my people Israel back into their land. That is exactly the thing America did after winning WWII.

The God hating liberals have been trying to rewrite history, ever since we ended it, calling us bullish and ungodly, even trying to blame us for starting it, and saying it was needless. I reckon they are angry that we won. Less and less every day since, we give God no credit or glory for any of it. God said it's a light thing to him and we broke both our arms trying to pat ourselves on the back for doing it. Regardless of which side you are on, when you take God out of the picture you are on the wrong side.

MacArthur at the end of WWII sent a message to Washington, D.C. and asked them to send him 2 thousand missionaries, that China and the east countries were on their knees. Do you think Washington showed any interest? No. We have failed to hold up God so many times till I am sure the opportunities are gone.

We threw him out of our own country, like the antichrist spirit always does we want to set in God's seat for ourselves. That will be the day. God says he is a jealousy God, said there was no God here when he came, no God with him now, and there will be no God here after he is gone. How much plainer can he get?

I've been studying about the hereafter, God, and what he has in store for us. He has given me many visions. I'm still studying them and learning. I study everything by the Word of God. I've found a lot of interesting things but found almost nothing about pain in the hereafter.

Jesus says a lot about misery, weeping and gnashing of teeth. A lot about a very unpleasant place of torment and a lake of fire but God's fire is altogether different from man, the devil, and the earth's fire. God's word says so in many places, look at the burning bush that God talked to Moses out of, it was burning but not consumed. Jesus baptizes with fire. At Pentecost they were covered with cloven tongues of fire. I've not found where they ever had to be treated for burns. God says evil is a destroying fire, but teaches the fire that Jesus brings is a refining fire. After suffering through a number of visions all very different one from another but I noticed trends or traits running much alike in them, a lot of traveling, not knowing where I was going or getting no place, all confusing and tiring, seeing a lot of things I didn't know anything about and could find nobody to help me or tell me anything. They all seemed just as lost as I was. After being grieved in my spirit I ask God what it was I was looking at, he said it was a godless world. To imagine an eternity in a world like that gives me the creeps.

Then I read in God's word about a point in time that God would have an angel to stand with one foot on land, one foot on the sea and say, "when the seven trumpets were finished there would be no more time." A little later said there would be no more pain, that former things were passed away, there would be no more sea. I am not trying to start a new doctrine, but I do not believe we should preach anything farther out than we can affirm by the Bible. I am told to be careful and not to distort or to wrest the Scriptures, not to add or take anything away from them, and I believe that is told to everybody.

It seems I started out on the subject of communications and keep getting off on rabbit trails. I have not figured out a way to stay off of them, so I'll just try to run some of them out. Man has kindly gotten stuck with words being his best and most used way of communication. Who would have thought man could have transported words, pictures, scenes, stories, messages and so many other things through the air and bounce them off of satellites, where there is no air and back all over the earth, and do it about instantly, and it be clearer than it would be if one was right there looking at it. And man thinks he did it without God? I guess that is the only way he can claim all the credit for himself is to deny that there is a God.

As for myself I refuse to believe that Jesus is a liar when he said we can do nothing without him. It explains so many things they cannot. Of course we could take it the way of so many others and start out with, "Oh, that's the way he said it, but here's the way he meant it".. fool; this is the kind of writings and false teachings I've been talking about. He said what he meant to say, and he meant what he said.

I would like to be an on looker when they put him on trial to trip him up and prove him wrong. The top debaters in Israel that were sent out from the Sanhedrin Court and High Priest to entrap Jesus in any word that he spoke didn't have very good luck at confusing or trapping him up. Of course they didn't have Bill O'Rilley or any other of the experts we have today. Neither are we factoring in how much smarter humans are today than they were in Jesus' day.

Jesus said he only spoke the words that the Father told him to speak, but of course our experts are smarter than God, if you don't believe that just ask one of them. They will get their chance to present their case, but I doubt if they will have very much to say. They should read the book of Job and save themselves a lot of trouble, and maybe erase a bunch of troublesome false hopes. I will not believe God has given any man more knowledge or talent than he has himself. Somehow my small mind cannot compute such a happening. Of course I've never been told by anybody that I have an expert mind in anything, but I have been told I am to give God glory in everything, and I believe that simply means to put him above in everything. We have nothing that he didn't give us, and we can do nothing without him. Puts me pretty small the way I understand it. And I don't see a thing wrong or degrading in admitting and facing just what I am. If that is too low, I will go to work at trying to bring it up a little bit, fair enough?

God is the giver of knowledge, wisdom and talent. Get to know him, learn how to follow him that is how he said to receive him.

CHAPTER 8

Hearing And Understanding God

I t is up to us to seek God and to study his word and to ask him for understanding when we need it. The big problem is not in the reading and the understanding, it is in the believing, men just do not want to believe God even when he is surrounded with proof every time he opens his eyes or draws a breath of air. This is why hell having to enlarge itself to receive all them that is rushing into it. You can blame God here all day long but when you get there you will only have yourself to blame. You're the only one you will walk into hell with.

I think I already mentioned how the Bible gave us the English language and made it the excepted language of the world. Just look what man has done to it against God's orders, he has added so many words to it, thousands in just my time, I have stated over and over we have many problems, but I am fully convinced that our educational system is without par in being the worst problem.

There must be thousands of reasons, one being the words along that my grandkids are expected to learn the definitions of are probably double what I was expected to learn when I was coming up through school about seventy years ago, not to mention the thousands of other confusing things that has been added to the curriculum since then. God is simple, and about every preacher I ever heard seems to be trying to make him as complicated and complex as he possibly can.

They are trying to force each child to learn everything, and all of them to learn the same thing, I don't see how that could make sense to anyone with a half sound mind and one eye. How much do they think they can stuff into their minds before they snap. In trying to teach them everything they are ending up teaching, maybe about ten per cent very well, and the rest somewhere around very close to nothing. I believe that is what some of them are calling dumbing down. Of course I would not expect a head shrink to agree with any of this, but the answer is to individualize the system a little bit and lean a little more toward allowing a kid to work toward a field that he is a little more qualified for, and maybe you can drum up a little interest in him, instead of letting the government name what he must work toward. Then to make their job easier, they just decide that every kid should learn and be interested in the same things. Don't that sound a lot like communism, even to you left headed God haters?

Ever since the Civil War when the government started getting more and more involved in our schools, every year they have went up on cost and down in quality. That should tell even our stupid government something. I believe their just a little bit too far gone.

In actuality it is not the government that's to blame it's the selfish, greedy, something for nothing, God hating people that would rather worship a good sounding lie when they know it's a lie than to hear the truth, I reckon it's because the truth is Jesus and he stands for responsibility. God said the world would hate him without a cause. He knew that before they crucified him. He knows everything. I challenge you to look at our schools. Every problem in our country has taken root there. As Obama says "Period".

Our teaching does not need improving, it's what they teach that needs to be completely turned around toward truth and away from lies. Look at our president for example, look good. If that is not enough, look at any politician or any lawyer. I know that all the extra brand new words that are not found in the Bible are needed to enhance our carnal language but God's language does not need them, and his dictionary does not include them directly, but I can assure you God knew all about every one of them before he gave them to us and they are covered in his word. And we would know a lot more about them if we knew more about how to study God's word, and the way to study it is also covered in his word. Of course it is hid from the wise and prudent of this world. God says if your one of them, to become a fool so you might be wise.

I just told you that it was hid from a smart carnal mind. If you don't seek God you will never find him, but God will not be the one that is remaining lost and stupid of the two of you. All of man's knowledge is made unto foolishness under God's wisdom. God gives his knowledge to them that have understanding, if you do not have understanding, he says to ask him for it, but never ask him doubting. Everything you try to run down to obtain from God, ends up at; "You must believe him." Once you start believing God it will open up a new window for you that will just grow and grow if you just keep believing, just don't doubt.

Doubt has a tendency to pull a curtain over God's window. God has told us to get understanding and he will give knowledge to them that have it. The word of God is life and it is always moving forward, progressing, and says woe to them that are at ease in Zion. I do not know exactly what he means by woe but I know enough to know I don't want any part of it. God's word also says there is no discharge in this war. It also gives us a list of the whole armor of God and told us to put it on and wear it.

I might add a saying here that you might be somewhat familiar with, "Ask not what your God can do for you, but what you can do for your God?".. .well people thought it was pretty great when another person used it in a similar situation, but not completely the same I guess.

The sword of the spirit, which is the word of God and is the only offensive weapon he gave us. The rest of them are defensive weapons, with nothing listed to cover our backs, which I take to mean he does not intend for us to turn our backs to Satan but fight him face to face he cannot stand against the Word of God. That is something I learned by experience and observation. He says the word of God is sharper than any two edged sword and separates the joints from the morrow and a designer of the thoughts and intents of the heart and is the battle weapon between the carnal and the spiritual, the heavenly and the earthly, the things from up above and things down here, the kingdom of God and the kingdom of man, surely you can get the picture, all in twos.

He says the kingdom of God suffereth violence and the violent take it by force. But people do not want to accept that scripture as true because they cannot accept God's kingdom as being defeated by the kingdom of this world. The kingdom that they think they are preaching cannot be defeated but by Jesus Christ. The problem is they are not preaching the kingdom of God but the kingdom of this world. It's the only kingdom they know so I guess they have to preach it. They need to read their Bible, or if they can't they need to get somebody to read it to them that can read. Did not Jesus tell his disciples that as long as he was here he was the light of the world but when he left didn't he say "ye are the light of the world." I can site probably fifty other scriptures that tell us plainly he turned the kingdom of God here on this earth, over to his people. He told us that he would move heaven and earth to help us hold on to it if necessary. But would not lift one little finger to hold it for us if we were just concerned about our self and not concerned about him or the kingdom and could not love a righteous God enough to put our faith or trust in him. We're to do everything to glorify God. Jesus said God could raise children of Abraham from these stones lying around, God says in a number of places the inhabitants of this world are nothing to him, and in at least one place I know, he said we were less than nothing. My point is where did we come into telling anybody we are anything in or for ourselves. If we cannot come to grips with, it is all God and nothing else. We will remain a pile of dirt, for God has said if I take my breath, or spirit, the same thing, back from you, you will go back to the dirt that you came from.

Of course a many of people believe that the one birth is enough for them, good luck!! That fleshly birth is never going to make it into the new heaven or new earth. How can we preach the true kingdom of God if we have not been born into it. I have read that to many times in the Bible to believe otherwise. Jesus says if we have not been born again we cannot see the kingdom of God. God has showed me that it is not him, but us, that is giving it away. Like our country, it is for sure it is going down, I told them so when Bill Clinton was first elected president, but it is not God or even Obama and the God hating liberal Democrats that are giving it away it is people that are called by his name.

When God said his people would stand and fight for him even to the death it makes me wonder where they are at, either they are so very few or maybe God just didn't know them very well. I am told that Dwight Moody, on his death bed said, "The world has yet to see what God would do for one man totally sold out to him." After seemingly spending most of his life with God removing spiritual mountains for him."

I'm the one that preaches that God is never wrong, so that should tell you where I stand. I say it is not God but us, that will not stand in the gap for one another or for the kingdom of God.

You would think by looking at us we don't even know that we are in a battle at all. Our president sort of knows we are in a war but only the one that Bush got us into, so he says. He has been preaching that he has brought nothing but peace since he has been in office, that is because he recognizes only one enemy, that is Christians holding on to their guns and God and their all Republicans, and all Republicans are them. I've decided only Democrats can figure that out, to understand it. I can't.

But I've figured out that man and Jesus are not talking about the same thing when they are talking about the word peace. The Word of God teaches we killed the prince of peace and there will be no peace till Christ gets back. Jesus said, my peace I give to you not as the world giveth, "let not your hearts be trouble." This is one of Hannity's favorite sayings. This says plainly, the peace that Jesus gives us is to keep our hearts from being troubled. How many people do you know that has a heart that cannot be troubled? Maybe I should ask that in a different way. How many people do you know who have the peace that Jesus Christ left here for us?

I'm kind of like David, and all the other writers in the Bible, they seemed to of had to live through and experience ever song and incident they wrote about, that helped them to write with feelings that we could receive with better understanding and would not have to suffer or experience the same costly mistakes.

I learned early in life and taught it to others as best I could, that experience may be the best teacher in the world, but it is the most costly and will defiantly take its toll on a body, Some of them you will not live through and life isn't long enough to get through them all. I believe that is one reason God developed books and writings and gave them to us, including the Bible so we could read and teach it and people and nations would not have to repeat all those things themselves, before they could know.

Of course if we refuse to believe, it will be of non-effect which is what our country is teaching, the Bible is out. That should explain to even the slowest of us why Satan, who came only to kill, steal and destroy, has so many possessed by him, hating the Bible and working so hard trying to destroy it. Do you know anybody it has personally attack or done any harm to? The reason they hate it is obvious, they are defiantly on the side of the world and it denies self and reveals both Satan and Jesus to the world.

They have tried to destroy the Word of God since Moses came down off the mountain with the ten commandments, and every time they turn around it is looking them in the face again and they haven't put one dent in it. No wonder they hate it so bad.

They have our whole government of the United States of America including everything that the government has a dime invested in, including our schools, forbidden to use a Bible or mention the name Jesus Christ in it or offering a silent prayer near it. Not allowing a cross to be sticking up in site on a mountain side. They have total control of ever thing but the church itself.

In and under the Carter Administration there was no less than 9 bills, introduced on the floor in Congress, that would allow congress to license and regulate preachers, do not tell me you don't know what that means. I have been trying to write this at around a third grade reading level for I do not want to be misunderstood, they are trying to take control of the church too.

In case you don't know what that means I will tell you. It means the government would have the authority to send their thuds down to your church any Sunday morning kick in your front door hand cuff your preacher and charge him with the crime of speaking against their favorite politician. If queer loving Senator Kennedy could have gotten his hate crime laws passed that he fought so hard for, they could have given that preacher 6 years in the penitentiary camp. And you wonder why I don't like Democrats?

Let me see if I got this right, your all right with people that are offended at the name of Jesus Christ teaching your children that it's fine for man to marry man or a horse and adopt children to raise and teach them to do these things, you have supported and voted for these people, have not opened your mouth against them probably rebuked and corrected people that have. Now here is what I would like to know from you, when you stand before Jesus, which you will, will you have the guts to stand there and try to tell Jesus that you were a Christian down here on earth and a soldier in his army?

He has told us to judge ourselves and he won't have to. You are right, I'll never be ask to set in judgment on you or nobody else, but nobody thanks God any more for that than I do. When they cannot destroy or put one black mark on the Word of God, then they send their college professors and people they graduated with the highest marks into lawyers, teachers, politicians and news casters to teach our kids and tell the world that the Bible is just a lie and they can prove it is a lie, and preach to the world of their peace, another lie, how is that working out for them? The entire world thinks that money is the answer for everything. They think it will buy freedom, contentment, friends, education, peace, God's favor, there is just no end to the list, and it's all a lie.

We spend trillions on top of trillions to purchase peace of mind.

How is that working out? No peace comes with money, if you're thinking that our money bought us all the power and greatness we have enjoyed these past few centuries maybe you should run for an office, for you are thinking like a stupid politician. This is why God said the love of money is the root of all evil, making Jesus the root of all peace. I do not need the world teaching me about peace and you do not need to send your children off to college to find peace, it is not there. The truth is we included God in our government and schools even in most of our homes and performed his will and it worked fairly well over the entire world.

Those kinds of principles had God paying our bills for us just like he said he would in the 28th chapter of Deuteronomy. The first 14 verses tell of the blessings to a people that will hearken unto his voice. The other 54 verses of that chapter tell of the curses they will receive if they don't. Which one do you think we are living under when we are looking up to and voting and supporting nothing but the worst of God haters that attack him every day?

The ones that thinks they are serving God, thinks he is one of Santa Clause's elves and is there to do their pleasure. They are both wrong and have not met nor do they know the righteous God of Israel. He is a terrible God, looking for a people that will tremble at his word. I did not say that, he did. You only have a choice of one of two ways. The ways are preordained, the choice is yours. The way with Jesus is the way of peace, but like everything else we do not see peace as God sees peace.

I think the most used words in president Carter's term was, peace and democracy. I told them then that he was making a dirty word out of democracy. Who can you sell it to today, who wants it? I know Carter has done a lot of work building and such till I guess some people thinks maybe God could not have gotten by without him. I thank God for everything he did that was good for humanity, but I think God could have made it through without him and I don't know one thing he gave to God's people, certainly not peace, the only thing them people he was dealing with calls peace is getting everything their way, and killing anyone that disagrees with them, maybe someone can write and inform me of something I don't know about, I'll be glad to read about it.

I'm not writing this from the world's point of view, but the best I can from God's point of view. They are far from being alike, hardly have any resemblance. God says if you have the peace of Jesus Christ you will be hated, persecuted, rejected and the wicked will even lay in wait to slay you. So if you cannot endure a few of these things probably no need to think seriously about living for and being used for God.

Jesus told his disciples when he sent them out to preach the word, when they entered into a town to enquire of a house that was worthy and stay there, if when you left you found the house to be worthy to leave your peace there with it, but if not to take your peace with you. I don't think Jesus was just talking about words, words or cheap, or even a small scene, I believe he was talking about something spiritual and real that the carnal cannot see or know anything about, and was not cheap, and money cannot buy, but cost heaven the greatest thing it had. And if you hate truth and righteousness, you hate it, for the god of this world does so. If you love this world's peace and think you've found it, take it with you and try to enjoy it for it will be the only heaven you will ever see.

We had a statesman helping in the war for independence, and the drawing up of the declaration of independence and the constitution for this great country, named Patrick Henry. Yes the same one our college professors, and their victims are trying to make into trouble making drunken rebels that upset the whole world that was living so peaceable worshiping governments for their gods, and trying to pin any other sorry name on any of the statesman that helped in our independence. Like womanizers, whisky makers, thieves, liars, and crooks.

Henry said in a speech that was held to be famous in my high school days, enough to be a requirement for memorization. Now it is a part of history they are desperate to try and bury. A line in it said "do we love peace or even life itself so much that we are willing to pay for it with bondage?"

Anybody with one spiritual eye can see why a man of the spirit of this world would hate a speech like that, leaning to much toward faith, or as they would say too religious, that's against the law of our land. Truth is if they cannot hear and understand the Word of God at least a little bit, they are guilty of vain jangling and do not know what they are trying to talk about. Where are the Christians at?

CHAPTER 9

"Woe Unto Lawyers And Judges Of The Earth"

Our politicians of today sure have a lot of room to talk, considering their track record, wouldn't you think? But a Christian better not say one word about his belief. Politicians are like, or worse, than anybody else, they think they can set in judgment on anybody and everybody, especially about God's word since they think they are setting in God's seat and know more than him, in a sense they are setting in the seat for God he says he puts them there, but in accordance to what we need and deserve for our own condition, and he will hold them responsible for every decision, and told us to not resist them. I think that clearly means physical, one place he says woe unto the judges of this earth, another place woe unto lawyers. They don't know God says his word has already judged everything and everybody and they are taking a huge risk to make a decision without knowing something about the Word of God, they better read some in it.

Judging is a word that seems to be accepted by every man to be permissible to be used against every other man, anytime or in any way at his will, but is unlawful and strictly forbidden for any man to use in any form or way against himself. I'm sure that God's word places it far between the two of them and neither one of them very close to being correct.

Though it is truly a very broad meaning word, because of so many different kinds of judgments and used in at least two kinds of opposite ways. There is them that are being judged, and them that are doing the judging. Both are being used at and on so many different levels, there is hardly one definition that fits different levels or situations. There is also judging in God's kingdom and judging in Lucifer's kingdom headed by the god of this world. They are far from being the same kind of judgment. Any time you use the word, it is deserving of some kind of looking into and explaining before any of it is applied, or any decision is made. I would recommend doing such things before anybody would be given authority to judge another man. It's called common sense.

Some rules God has laid out is, there is no unrighteousness to be used in any kind of judgment, no favoritism toward any side, no unjustice of any sort but truth and fair. What fair means, what is fair for everybody that is concerned? No man is to judge another man's servant. The one judging should be qualified, responsible and given the authority to do the job as long as he fills these qualifications. I believe that would cover most all of God's requirements, That alone means no man will be able to judge a call for God, to say if any other man is to go up or to go down. God says just don't say it.

That should just about cover and explain about any question that would come up, if we can just receive what God says. He says we should judge ourselves and he would not have to judge us, and he will judge us with the same judgment that we judge others by, and if we judge nobody, then we will not be judged. The word has already judged us all. All we have to do is study it.

Just like everything else man gets it backwards to God and thinks he can judge everybody, and nobody can judge him. Knowing it or not, he is making judgment calls on himself all day long, every day. If we will tend to that, we will be too busy to judge another man, and that would settle a lot of problems for everybody. God says he is busy at judging every day, so I'll try to leave all the judging to him that I can.

I sternly believe in judging everything by the Word of God but that has a lot of definite requirements, first, you better be doing a lot of studying in the Bible, and have scripture to affirm any scripture you use. If someone does not believe the Bible then what does he have to affirm anything with unless you have the object your discussing right there to look at. But I believe that would be judging by appearance and Jesus said not to do that. Seems Jesus just about denies his people to do any carnal judging in the carnal but has commanded us to constantly judge with and in a righteous judgment. This fact along should reveal the importance for each of us in obtaining some understanding of righteousness and for understanding of judging for we are commanded to mix and use them both together.

The one thing that becomes the plainest and most obvious in doing this is to see how, when you take the Word of God out of it, like the God hating liberals are doing to our country, in a big way, you don't have nothing left but chaos. God has promised no protection, no support, no blessing of any sort to chaos, but destruction. I guess what I'm trying to say is it's not very sensible to argue with an unbeliever, especially one that does not want to hear truth, do not use a scripture quoted contrary to another scripture, better study and see which one you are looking at wrong, and be able to explain them both. God says to establish every word out of the mouth of two and three witnesses. And that don't mean go to your nearest bar to find somebody to agree with you, it means to find two and three places in God's word to back it up, if you are quoting it right they will be there.

I've already explained much about how communication is our first and probably the most important factor involved in dealing between God and man, or anybody else. I served better than 4 yrs. in the U.S. army, most of it in the infantry artillery. They taught us the artillery had three missions, to shoot, move and communicate, if we failed in one, we were dead. We communicate with words, sounds and signals that means words. Now is where false teachers and false prophets come to play. God has warned us much about both and give us many ways to identify them, and how they would be more active in the last days.

I believe they are very plainly here and plentiful, one of the signs of end times. I've never heard of so many smart people thanking they have figured out great knowledge on how God is going to handle these last days, what and when. Like a rapture and why and when they must be one, who cares? He has told us everything we need to know and I'm sure he doesn't need my advice, and doubt it if he needs anybody else's either. He sure didn't tell me about a rapture in his word, now I've been told by a lot of preachers, and read about it in Dake's Bible. One of the most tremendous works maybe I ever saw about the Bible. I've read my bible through and through, but I still have not read in my Bible about a rapture. I guess I'm just not very good at reading I've not found yet where God's children are going to leave this earth and fly out to somewhere called heaven.

I read where Jesus cast some into outer darkness where he said there was weeping and gnashing of teeth. But I don't believe they were his people, I believe our astronauts tells us that it is dark out there unless the sun hits something and reflects light, something like that, strange to say the least. I reckon they all agree that you don't have to have wings to fly.

Anyway I'm far more interested in telling God's people about the battle we are in. It's a battle for our souls and we are playing for keeps, and if them God hating liberals like Tom Brokaw and most of the others cannot see that the Viet Nam war and WWII was playing for keeps, and calling it a bullish, needless act for winning WWII and making our boys criminals that was trying to win the Viet Nam war and would not let them win the war because they were afraid some of their Christian killing brothers might get hurt. Israel is the only enemy Obama and them have in the Middle East, besides our soldiers. And we expect them to recognize the battle they got going on with the spirit of God, and if you cannot recognize it, it's because you are on the wrong side, don't think you are not involved for God didn't give you that choice, God said the flesh is warring against the spirit, and said he is a spirit, Jesus said if you are not with us you are scattering abroad so you might as well wake up and get on an uniform you are already in the war and as I've already told you the Word of God is the only sword we are going to get to fight with, but it is enough, Jesus has already won the war at Calvary. God says to wake up, blow the trumpet, sound the alarm and put on the whole armor of God every piece of it is spiritual and light. It is listed in the 6th chapter of the book of Ephesians. False prophets are the most damnable thing in the kingdom of God, without a doubt.

Look for truth, Jesus Christ is the truth, the way, the life, he is all of it and don't be offended in him. The man that is offended in truth is a cursed man, anybody who is minding the things of the flesh is opposite of and contrary to God. And there is no other end for him but destruction, it has already been declared. Why fight on the wrong side of a war that has already been lost? Because it is wrong and built on a lie.

Them that have accepted the mark of the beast or the number of a man have already given up and said, "Who can fight against this man?" They should read on in the book, it says that Jesus Christ and his chosen ones can fight against him, and will win. Of course them that cannot believe, can't see that and cannot have it, I believe it is called victory, and everyone that has not their name written in the lamb's book of life will follow the antichrist and will worship him. That is the spiritual mark that the carnal cannot see.

The spirit can see it from across the world. God says all worship that does not touch God, the devil receives. That means if you are not worshiping the truth, you are worshiping the Devil. The word worship means giving honor to something. The Devil is a copier and swore he would rise above the most high and set his seat in the north places and receive the worship of the congregation. He will carnally make it down here on Earth for a short time with the vast majority of its inhabitants that just cannot give in to love righteousness more than themselves and choose to believe a good sounding lie when anybody with half a mind would know it is a lie.

Look at our president, the best example God has ever put on the face of this earth of the very antichrist, anybody who did not know he was nothing but a liar had to be operating under the shoe soul of their very minds, with no contact with God's spirit. Of course anybody that will take the time to read the Bible can know what happened, God said in 9th psalms he would turn into hell any nation and any people that would dare to forget him, that implies they once knew him, I don't believe there has been another nation on earth that knew God any better than this nation has known God. Now I cannot with the wildest spot in my imagination wrap my mind;;; wrap nothing, I cannot run it by my mind, the hate I see in this country for the Lord Jesus Christ, it's too big. Just plain old deep in the heart, mind and soul hatred, it is beyond belief.

God said he would send strong delusions to believe a lie so all them might be dammed that do not love truth, look at who we have put to running this country, look at our lawmakers, look at our lawyers, look at our courts, look at our schools. You would be hard pressed to find an ounce of truth in any of it. Even our churches don't look much better. I see no fear of God in about anything you can point at. Jesus Christ is the truth and the truth is Jesus Christ they can hate all they want to but they will not change one letter in that statement. So when they hate Jesus they hate truth, when they hate truth they hate Jesus Christ. You can never separate them. When anyone puts their trust in a lie they will be destroyed, we cannot even be wrong and get by. Paul warned of the end times when they would not endure sound doctrine, I believe that means nothing more than they will insist on believing a good sounding lie, rather than truth because it is easier and feels so much better to them, no worries, besides it looks profitable.

I guess that is good as long as you can just ignore the consequences too, if you're never held responsible who cares? God has made it plain that there will not be one soul allowed to escape receiving a just reward for all his works and actions, except through Jesus Christ, we will see some day, that God is not like man, he does not lie. A quality which man cannot attain to, this fleshly condition is gone beyond hope.

Not all the laws God gave in the Old Testament, not all the blood that was shed by millions of animals and millions of God's people could make one man righteous, no not one. Only the blood of Jesus can make a man righteous, and Jesus is truth and comes in no other form. People are so foolish as to think by comparing themselves to everybody else they can make themselves righteous by their works or looks or pride or anything they can come up with. Not even their own blood is sufficient. They might as well get used to it they can both humble themselves and except the blood of Christ or else.

One's bank account will only affect him not God. In these last days God said everything that can be shaken will be shaken, it is a trial period for God's people, he said he would have a tried people, said I'll prove you, if you love me or if you don't. We might as well make up our minds, the sooner the better. Choose the side we want to be on. The ones trying to ride the middle fence is some of the most miserable people on the earth.

This does not mean if you sin you're on your way to hell for Jesus knows we were born into sin so he paid for all the sins so nobody will go to hell for their sins, but will go to hell for not repenting and not believing and not excepting the way of Jesus Christ. We will suffer consequences of sin, but Jesus will forgive you over and over until our hearts get harden and our conscious are seared with a hot iron and we have no more conscious of sin, then we are gone, not because Jesus threw us out but because the spirit of God cannot draw us anymore. Like so many have become already. Judge ourselves, are we willing to be tried and chastised?

CHAPTER 10

There Is A Way To Make Things Right

I've heard it preached all my life that one sin is just as bad as another, that sin is sin, and there is no such thing as a little sin, and many more such strong remarks saying the same thing. They get it all, as far as I can tell from one scripture with no backing to preach it so strong or to that extent, it's where Paul said if you Transgress one law you are guilty of the whole law for sin is sin, he did not say there is no such thing as a little sin. He didn't say a lot of other things I've heard them claim, Paul was talking from God's point of view, not from our point of view.

It's a sure thing with God that sin is sin, Jesus paid for all the sins of the world, at one dying, he did not weight them out one at a time and pay so much for each one he paid for our sins and sin was paid for, so if we sin all we do is confess our sin and ask him, he is faithful to forgive us and that is that as far as God is concerned. He doesn't even remember it against us.

But let us look at it from our point of view, remember I said in the beginning of this book that everything is what it is according to where you are looking at it from, this is a classic case, it is just a light thing to God to forgive us for our sins, he has done and done that and he can forget it, but it's not the same thing with us we have to live with the consequences and be overcomers. God will help us but he will not change the world for our convenience.

There's a lot of old sayings that make me realize that people of old was not as dumb as we like to think they were, one of them was, "if you make your bed you will sleep in it," about the same thing I'm saying here. Let's say a couple gets together and have a baby before their married, oh, they have repented many times, and been sorry, and wept many times. Do you think God should put the baby back where it came from? That is the kind of God most people are looking for and disappointed when God don't fit that pattern. God says we should serve him, not him serve us, because he knows the truth and the truth is right. But we love a god that will lie to us to make us feel good and go to hell rather than face the truth. I believe anybody that would open their eyes and take one look that he could see why our God is not that stupid.

Can you imagine a world with God a slave to seven billion people? Of course each person can only view himself as being his own god, just wants the power, he could not ever visualize everybody having God for a slave. I find about every person thinks alone them lines, don't sound to smart to me. I would not want the job if he tried to give it to me.

Take David's sin with Bathsheba for another example. He got the wife of one of his 30 mighty men with child, he sent and had him brought in off the battle field to try to have it covered up, when that didn't work out he sent him back to the battle with orders to have him killed and then took his wife for his own wife. Then without knowing it David pronounced a death sentence on himself. But God said no, David, I'm not going to kill you, but you have released a sword and turned it lose in your own house and that sword will never depart from thine house. God killed the baby to keep the sword down some so David would not have to do it later, I assume. I noticed God's word called the first son, of Uriah's wife. David took Bathsheba to wife making it legal and proper I suppose, now that Uriah was dead, but it did not remove the sword that was in David's house, I suppose until today. Since God said it would never remove. God referred to the next son David and Bathsheba had as of David's wife and made him the next, and most famous king of them all.

David went on to see at least two of his sons kill two of his other sons, one of his sons rape one of his daughters, one of his sons tried to kill David to get his throne and had to be killed and I'm sure many other things happened. Our sins may not affect God much different in size but I would say it's quite a different story when it comes to us. We reap what we sow that is a New Testament law and has not been repealed. There is an old song that comes to mind here, "Sin is to Blame, Sin is to Blame."

One of the main reason it affects us so is, it don't effect just us but it effects everybody around us and everybody we come into contact with even everybody that hears about it, sometimes even 50 years later. Sometimes just something we say can be that lingering and that effective, think about it, no wonder God warns us to be so careful, especial around kids. They seem to pick up on everything and remember about all of it too. So when I say consequences that could be covering a very big field.

Paul said Able was testifying to us tell today, that is just about the length of all of time that God has given us. Of course you could never tell O'Rilley and Goldburg that for they know better. If you don't believe me just ask them. I'm just not very convinced that they know anything about the time on earth 4 to 5 billion years ago. I'm positive they would have a hard time proving anything. I guess it would sound a little like double jeopardy to a lawyer to pay for our sins here and to pay later in hell but it's really not, for you don't go to hell for sins. Jesus died for them. You will go to hell for neglecting Jesus Christ and that is all you have to do. It would sound a little unfair if it was not made so plain and so easy, that instead it sounds too good to be true.

I think that the hard part is to deny self and surrender entirely to Jesus, but we better realize that this flesh and blood cannot dwell in heaven with God. A spirit does not have flesh and blood. That is a problem and if we cannot accept that, then heaven would not be any different when we got there than the earth is today. God would just have to let us kill off each other or kill us off himself. That sounds like a good deal since we well know we are going to die down here. Who can deny that or pretend like it isn't so?

Does this country believe God is such a fool after the way they have hated him here, that if he takes them to heaven all of a sudden they will love him, I think not, he says if you cannot love man down here, made in the image of God, whom you have seen how can you love God whom you have not seen. If you will read your Bible closely it will tell exactly who and what part of man to love, Bible says love not the world or the things of the world, for the love of the father is not in them. I do not have to wrest that scripture one single bit to understand it clearly and all the rest of the Bible will back it up over and over.

The part of a man that is in, for, by, and of this world and loves this world, I am commanded not to love. The part of a man that is in the image of God like he was created in, that is to say with the righteousness of Jesus Christ, you are one with that part, members one of another. If you cannot recognize righteousness that is like saying you do not know Jesus Christ. This is what I mean when I'm always saying know the spirit you are of, and know the spirit you are talking to, if you don't know it, I'd say that is almost lost.

God says we should walk in the spirit of God and it knows everything even the deep things of God. My mind, or even my whole head is not big enough to contain even a pinch of that kind of knowledge, it would blow it up. But I have the spirit of God and learning more every day to put my complete trust in it. That is called growing in the Lord.

I'll repeat myself again and say the biggest problem we have on this Earth is in what we are teaching. God says to let him that teaches in the word communicate unto him that teaches in all good things. It also says that he that labors in the word is deserving of double honor, the only reason he give for making Abraham the father of all that believed by faith was, "I know Abraham, he will teach his children to teach their children's children that my laws will not die."

What did Jesus and all his Disciples all do? They were all teaching the word of God, most of them died for it. I could go on and on with scripture but I believe I've made my point, the Bible puts a lot of emphases on teaching, I believe we should too, we are told to. But I would agree with the most of you, I do not know very many preachers that I would want to be the teacher of my kids and grandkids. And if the government gets the authority to license clergymen I would not know any. So we need to put the Bible back in our schools and homes and pay more attention to what they are teaching than we do to the teachers.

They are teaching our children there is no difference between a man and a woman, you can tell them for me that Bill Wilson said they are lying. Jesus said there is no such thing as male and female in the spirit, and we see no such thing as marriage or reproduction in the spirit, but when men began to multiply on the earth the sons of God saw the daughters of men that they were fair so they took them to wife and renown men and giants were born upon the earth. If you read the creation in Genesis you can notice that God created a female after he created a male, to keep man from having to live alone, and for a helpmate. I read where he repented forever making either of them for it didn't work out very well at all. I've never read where he made female to lead.

I'll try not to start a war here, I think ones already started but I intend to just stay with the Bible and let God worry about the consequences I trust he can handle anything that jumps up. Now that sounds a little contradictory to what Jesus said about male and female, but let me assure you there is no contradiction anywhere in this Bible, which is one of the first lines from a false teacher. And you will never tell a man that believes God that there is. If you can then he no longer believes God.

In the books of Peter and Jude both tell of angles that left their estate, probably with Lucifer when he was threw out of Heaven and to the earth. They had left their estate in heaven and landed on earth when God created it. When the fallen angles saw the women they were fair and they had been given no such comfort, so they left their habituate and moved into a human habituate but it completely polluted the race for what God had intended it to be.

Even though the spirits were not created with male and female they plainly had the ability to change their habituate but when they did God reacted with the biggest act of judgment that we have on Record. He cast the angles that chose to live ungodly into hell in chains of darkness. These angles did not have to be from Lucifer they could be just as likely from God's angles that left their estate but either way God acted very quickly and with the harshest judgment that we have record of. They are suffering today the vengeance of an eternal fire. God shortened down the length of life he give man and swore he would not always strive with man.

Later he destroyed the whole world save eight souls and an ark load of animals. He destroyed Sodom and Gomorrah for the same crime, sexual perversion, for an ensample that man would not live ungodly any more. Anybody, again, with common sense and one eye should be able to see clearly why Christians cannot buy the alternate way of living that the God hating left are forcing upon us. That I will die before I will accept it. But Christians everywhere are not heeding the warning and getting overcome with the same ungodly sin of leaving our habituate and volunteering to go into sexual perversion, the give up of God, the last straw. God has warned sternly that if he spared not the angels that did this that he would not spare us for the same thing. Where are the believers?

The flood did not clean the entire earth, for David had to kill one of the giants, and a tribe is talked about long after the flood, Israel just about annihilated the tribe of Benjamin for the same sin God called it trampling the blood of Christ under foot. Changing their habituate must have been the most ungodly thing committed in God's sight. It is no marvel that a spirit can occupy another habituate, the Holy Ghost over shadowed Mary to have Jesus. If they can do that then could they not also have the power to do the opposite and take on the form of a woman and fool the men? It is obvious that they preferred the roll of a male I guess because of the dominate roll God gave to the male, and he did. Back then I'm sure it was easier to fool the women than the men, to read about Adam, Sampson, Ahab and Solomon, you could easily think otherwise, but the Bible does not teach they were fooled it just teaches they foolishly chose to go with their woman.

That was back then, but I see a great change taking place, the Bible warned us in many places and in many ways, in Isaiah God said in the last days our women would rise up and they would rule over us and our children would be our oppressors and princes. Women are taking over in every area I know anything about, we started out being taught that they are equal, now it's they are superior just suppressed. Don't ask me where they are going, ask them. Or somebody that can read a women's mind and that sure isn't me.

If you have a preacher or teacher telling you that there is male and female in the spirit world, you can tell him he is lying, and I don't care if he is a liberal Democrat. The whole male race is getting so girley some of them are getting so that they cannot look at themselves and figure out which one they are a woman or a man. I would say they need help, but I would have no idea how to help them. It's obvious that our college professors, politicians, lawyers, or even doctors have no answers for them. They don't know what makes our children take guns to school and shoot one another dead then kill themselves. Don't you reckon it might be another fallen spirit changing habituates? I don't know which one to blame and don't know anybody in the carnal world that would do anything about it if you told them where all the blame lays. But I believe starting to face up to the truth and began to teach truth just might be the answer, God says it is. Don't know why anybody would want to look any farther for the ones to blame than to the ones that produced them. The Bible says we will reap what we sow and if children aren't seeds that we have sown just mark me off here and call me done. Hope we can part as friends.

I said some of this about the Colorado shooting, which seemed to be the one that kicked it off to a start after David Wilkerson had warned us for a few years that it was coming. But of course who wants to be found to be so stupid as to listen to a religious freak like that, they rather listen to a smart man of god like Rev. Jessie Jackson or Rev.

Al Sharpton, now they have THE WORD OF THE LORD. I pray the Lord forgives me for writing that.

All the TV Stations were filled with the smartest people they could come up with, about all you could see on TV for weeks, trying to figure out why it happened and how to keep it from happening again. Did they come up with anything? NO. Some of the things they would suggest were so stupid it would make a grown man want to cry, something I've always said I hated most to see is a grown man crying. But they could about push my button. Even though not a one of them ever come close to the answer, my family and church had to put up with me giving it to them about every time I saw or heard them on TV. Being, if them kids would have been raised up sternly in the fear and admonition of the almighty God you could not have paid them enough to have taken a gun into that school room, not to mention shooting thirteen of their class mates. That's the difference in having taken God out of our homes and our schools, in that order, and teaching our children against him. We are looking at the results. As our president says, period..

CHAPTER 11

Wars And Rumors Of Wars

I've had a lot of principles I held up to myself from my youth till today and have changed a very few of them, none of them without reason. One of them is I don't want to start a war, (or fight as it was called before the Democrat party started telling us how to think and talk), with nobody, but if anybody insist on having one with me I'm going to do everything within my power to end it, and I'm a very sore and poor loser. They might consider that.

The war with women that Obama has started, is like Christians with Moslems, trade wars with other countries, government with our Christians, whites against minorities, I could go on and on for a couple of pages, most all of them are pushed on us from politician's minds so they can play like heroes and they do not care about the casualties as long as they can score political points.

Obama is the worst that I ever saw or can find in the pages of history. God put him up there, for God has turned us over to a reprobate mind. We will believe a lie and be dammed because we do not love truth. He has sent us strong delusions to believe a lie.

He told me a few days before the first election of Obama that he was going to do it and he wanted me to know it was his doings and to not get in his way. I backed off of the election process so abruptly my friends thought I just completely quit them, that was not so. I kept right on preaching the truth just as hard as I ever did but I backed out of anything physical. Not that I thought I would make a difference I just didn't want God to think I was in his way. I take God seriously whether I understand him or not. Of course I understand much better now than I did then. I was mighty glad that Arkansas did not vote for him and very few of our neighboring states did. I felt like the word of God that I was preaching made much difference.

Has not congress declared a war on God? Has not the Muslims declared a war on America, Christians and Jews? Even to bombing us all, time and again. Every time a Bill O'Rilley's staff member or anybody on his show says anything toward tighten down on anything on the left. Bill comes up with "Oh, you want to start a war"?? Looking like he is about to go into shock or something. I'm about sure he must wear padding between his knees to keep them from bumping together from fear. It must be painful, looking out for all of us. Sometimes I wonder if I need it from somebody that is that scared of the left headed God haters. Just lately I believe I been seeing a little bit of improvement in his courage that has always been there when he has been pushed a little. Guess I owe him a little apology.

I appreciate all the good that Bill O' does, and it is much. If he goes into shock all I know to do is maybe lay him down, elevate his feet, put a wet towel on his face, cover him with a blanket, try to keep him warm and calm, I'm not a very good doctor you know.

God did not tell us to be a floor matt for false profits, teachers of false religions, or even the fearful to wipe their feet on, even if it cost us our lives. And I'm told that it will come to just that. Where is the Christians at, that Jesus called to stand up to this world that he said would hate us? I'm sure that he is looking for them too. We need to stand up before we lose all our liberty in this world. Someone said, a long time ago that all that has to be done for evil to take over, is for good men to do nothing, when my liberties are being taken I call that evil. So when someone tells you that there is no difference between a man and a woman, and they can each marry whatever they want to, including a horse if they choose that nothing is wrong with it. That is not just a lie. It is a very evil lie. God says to put them to death, on all three counts. Remember God says he speared not the angles that left their habitation and he would not spear us either, He did not just condemn the ones that tell a lie, but the ones that help a lie, the ones that loves a lie, the ones that believe a lie, and the ones that has pleasure in a lie, is deserving of death. I have trouble in separating the words please and pleasure, sounds to me like they cover the same things. God says there is no part of a lie in him, so I'm determined to have as little to do with liars as possible. They are already dead to God, how do you put someone to death that is already dead? I haven't figured that out yet except to know why God calls so many out so early, it's not safe to mess with God even if you are volunteering to do his dirty work he will finish with you and let you go to hell if you hate him and refuse to fear and love him. If you are afraid to stand up for God yourself, at least give some support to them that do, instead of attacking them for your own profit, which is vanity and evil. Maybe if we just used our voice a little once in a while, now and then if we claim to be a Christian, unless God has turned you over to a reprobate mind yourself. God says you are if you are speaking for such things as homosexuals, same sex marriage and that complete line of thinking. I'll not take time and space here to name them, use your own mind a little and read your Bible, it is very plain about such things. Carnal freedom is not liberty.

The Bible, God's Word, and anything containing the Spirit of God, speaking against the reprobates, as God calls them in the book of Romans 1st Ch. have their own god. Lucifer, rider of the white horse in the 6th Ch. of the book of Revelations, which is a god in the spirit world as Jesus is, except Lucifer turned against God and was threw out of heaven while trying to overthrow God. He wanted to set in his seat to take control of everything. So there was war in heaven which we are told about, but not given much detail, for a very good reason. Like everything else about God's business, we do not have the capacity to retain it and could never understand it anyway. That is the reason why we just have to trust God or else, as Peter said, Lord, where would we go?

Lucifer is in charge of the earth but God has changed his name to many better fitting names, like devil, serpent, dragon, son of perdition, Satan and many more. Names denote character with God. When God changes their character he usually changes their names. I was amazed to find that Lucifer, which means son of light, or morning star, was only mentioned in the Bible by that name one time. Apparently God didn't think it was a very fitting name after pride was found in him and he had completely changed his character. If we believe God, we know it happened and we can go from there.

The 14th chapter of Isaiah is just a plain short record of the rise and fall of Lucifer from next to God in Heaven to the earth and the total pits of hell after the battle of Armageddon, which I hope you can read now with a little better understand. He will be imprisoned there for the one thousand year reign of Christ on this earth, and then he will be released again and allowed to go organize and gather from all the nations of the earth them that did not like the righteous rule of the lord Jesus Christ, ruled from Jerusalem with an iron hand, called the millennial reign. Lucifer will gather everybody that does not love righteous living and a perfect rule over all the earth and convinces them, they have a last perfect opportunity to join him, and obtain their independence that they fought for all their lives.

He thinks they can do it by surrounding Jesus and all his saints at their camp in Jerusalem and convinces the largest army ever formed on earth they can eliminate them. Remember Lucifer is their god. The spirit is the only side that can revile this to you.

I believe the same people that will not believe God today will not believe God then. Here is the thing that the carnal mind cannot grasp. The people that do not believe the Bible today will not be the same people that God will be dealing with then but the spirit will be the same and will look and be the same thing with God. It is just the spirit that matters with God the people are just slaves to the spirit they lend the members of their bodies too. They will count only to themselves. And will reap in judgment with the spirit that they held on to for the short time they had on this earth. Whatever time you are on this earth, it is like a puff of smoke to God, even less to the Antichrist spirit. All the spirits will account only to God. That is why the people that do not know what spirit they are of are blind and actually know nothing. They will not have a clue to what they are getting into, are even who they are working for. I can tell you who you are working for if you cannot acknowledge a spirit. You are working for yourself and your spirit that God breath into you that made you into a living soul for a short time. And I can tell you everything you will receive on judgment. Next time you lose a close friend or love one, after you have put them away, look around and see what is missing or what they took with them. That is assuredly their reward from this world. The only thing that will be added to them when they reach eternity will be spiritual and they cannot see or believe or even acknowledge there is such a thing as a spirit, or in the old English word, a ghost. That is just foolishness to a carnal mind. What do you expect to hear God say when you get there, April fool maybe.

Why they don't know what spirit they are of and cannot see that the same spirit now will be the same spirit then, I don't know. But I think this last war will be the shortest and the biggest battle ever recorded, Satan will be cast alive into the lake of fire. All of his followers and everyone whose name is not written in the lamb's book of life will be cast in with him. That is the judgments that all will receive that do not know and have the spirit of God.

CHAPTER 12

God Can Be Understood, Only In The Spirit

To tell the story of the Bible from the day of the Lord forward is hard, if not impossible to explain, it comes under the question they ask Jesus, when was he going to turn back to the Jews and his people. Jesus simply replied, it is not for you to know the times and the seasons that the Father has reserved unto himself. Let's do a little research and explaining here.

To start with it is completely ridiculous to see this from the position that God does not know these things, or he is just withholding something good from us. He has given us a plain negative answer to both thoughts, so let us look somewhere else in the Bible for the explanation of the reason for that answer.

Their question there in the first chapter of the book of the Acts of the Apostles, ask by his apostles, I believe is concerning the same thing the latter Christians are referring to when they are speaking of what they call a rapture. Jesus saying it was not for them to know the times and the seasons of these things. Do they think they can go ahead of God and reason these things out when God said plainly that it was not for us to know? I believe they have holes in their head, the carnal mind is not capable of reasoning the spirit nowhere that it didn't intend to go in the first place. He has told us the carnal mind is emulous to God, does not know a thing about God, thinks the things of God are foolishness and cannot understand anything about God, and has somewhere between very little and no communication with God. He does not need to explain anything to a carnal minded person which has separated himself from God, despised God, and does not trust him or believe anything he says, and certainly will not honor God or worship him. Even though there is no need to tell them, truth is, none of these facts are the reason for that answer Jesus gave them. God is not the kind of God to use our sins, our curiosity, our ignorance against us if we will just acknowledge our condition and trust and believe God he has made his arm bare to us, told us all things and declared the end from the beginning, but if we will not acknowledge our condition, trust, receive and believe God we have no capacity to retain any understanding. We cannot receive or handle any part of that knowledge for God, to help him or his people, but would use it for the opposite purpose and use everything to try to destroy anything about God and his people. That is what a spirit apart from God will do.

This will not happen within the body of Christ. God has told us and showed us an example, saying if he spared not his angles that deserted their inheritance, and left their habitation, set themselves apart from God and the habitat they were created to inhabit, but cast them into hell and are suffering the vengeance of an eternal fire. He will not spear us either.

As far as I can find we have no record of any people that at this time have been cast into and suffering an eternal fire of hell, other than these sons of God that left their habitat. And we have been assured that if he spared not these angles that did this that he would not spare us that did the same thing.

I cannot answer for anybody but myself with no more than the Word of God and my opinion. But my opinion will be expressed from and upon the Word of God as much as I possibly can accomplish that.

But as far as the opinion that, you can have your opinion and I can have mine and we can just go our ways and do the best we can and we will be all right, is worse than not having an opinion at all, for we are not given that luxury in any form, or he would not have said for us to work diligently to make our calling and election sure. No need to work to make our calling and election sure if all we have to do is just to except that it is sure.

But any time you bring up an opinion or just the word opinion you open up a rabbit trail that looks like a wide road and I cannot resist this one now, but I promise I will get back to the reason Jesus gave that answer that I was talking about and was trying to explain, as soon as I can. I reckon everybody is entitled to an opinion, I think everybody has one, making it about the cheapest thing I know about, that's just fine, but opinions should stop as soon as truth comes in. I find I have to deal with this with about every person I have to talk to about any subject. I find most of them is positioned to be for or against something and will be trying to add to whichever side he is on, if he has the least bit of interest in it, with his opinion.

Religion and politics is among the most controversial subject of all. Admit it are not, I believe about everybody has a deep interest and concern in them both. If they didn't have they could discuss them without getting so upset every time they are brought up in conversation. How many times have you heard it said that friends should never discuss religion and politics? I had a person say that to me once, I corrected him and said no, they should be able to discuss them both and keep an open mind and a calm spirit and stick to truth and what they know to be true and things would work out just fine. They could both express their opinions and they could walk away with their opinions and still be just as happy as they pleased, and possible both could be a little better informed.

That's not likely to happen for neither one is satisfied with allowing the other one to do that. People are like magicians, each one carrying around a bag of dirty tricks, wishing to practice and perfect some of their favorites at every opportunity. They are developed for the purpose to deceive.

Let us use a religious denomination for an example. I've about got myself whipped maybe 3 or 4 times over saying I thought Glen Beck was a Christian, I mentioned this another place in my writing but I intend to make a different point this time, on how they bring about their argument with their tricks that I see everywhere. They say he cannot be a Christian because he is a Mormon. I don't guess they have enough sense to know it but they just set themselves in the seat of God and sent every Mormon to hell on the spot, nothing else to consider in their judgment, done deal. I bet if you're a Mormon, your glad that them being God is just in their imagination and can be dismissed as their ignorance for that is all that it is, you have not been sent to hell just yet, but wait, he has not finished yet, there is more. If they can put a name on anything they can turn their attack onto the name, now it's not on the person or thing anymore, but on the name, which he thinks he has done. Trick #1. Then they will look into the whole Mormon Church to find everything they can, and pick the best or worst Mormon, depends on which way you are looking at it from, to judge and start tearing down the whole Mormon Church denomination. Trick #2, (these tricks work for them against any denomination or anything else, so don't get hung up here on the Mormon church for I do not intend to reflect my opinion on or of the Mormons or to effect yours. They are irrelevant to anything I'm trying to say here).

They will instantly pick the farthest out one, to make him look like the whole church, and the direct representative of everyone in the whole church. Trick #3, so now they have justified themselves to send him to hell. I'd like to ask who give them that authority in the first place. That is where they start to get mad upset and start preparing to give me a whipping, how dare me to take the liberty to question his opinion. He has the liberty to send the whole Mormon Church to hell, along with Glenn Beck cause he just tied him to it. I told him I had never heard Beck preach any Mormon doctrine. He told me I was the most stupid person he ever had to talk to. Now, (trick #4) is the time when they get to a boiling point and blow over.

I have written about knowing the spirit you are of and the spirit you are talking to. This is a good place to illustrate a little of what I was saying, I knew far back in the story that this person was not coming off of the spirit of God. Even when his mind had him seated in God's seat his actions had him serving the spirit of the devil who came to do nothing but kill, steal and destroy, how hard is that to see? I'm not talking about one or two incidental happenings. I am talking about a pattern that our schools are teaching and has the whole world trying to perfect. These are not all the tricks they have. They have huge bags of them. If you want to hear them just listen to or lawyers and college professors, if you want to see them at work just look at our best politicians if you want to see the results, just look across our great country and all the people, and look good at the shape both of them are in.

Then if that don't show you something we should all know what Jesus was talking about when he told us he came to blind or carnal eyes so we might be able to see. If we believe what we were looking at was truth then Satan has blinded our minds and I'd say there is very little hope for us. From what the Bible teaches, the light of the saving gospel shines in through the mind into the heart. Jesus is the light and life, is the same as God, and thereby we are saved. But if Satan can blind our minds, so it seems like God considers we see with our minds more than the eyes, then the light cannot shine through to our hearts and we cannot be saved and remain blind.

Can these God hating servants of Lucifer, the earth's spiritual god, do that? I'll let you ponder on the answer to that one a while. Apparently politicians can do that, look where they are sending our Christian nation, remember when Obama said "This is not a Christian nation" and a majority of our people loved it. All the rest of the world loved it, and you know Obama would not lie, under the threat of his life. O'Rilley says you cannot call him a liar, of course O'Rilley can say that the Bible, Jesus and God are telling a lie, but when he was confronted with it he said he did not call Jesus a liar, (Tick #5), you've got to look at this from the same position they are looking at it from, It will look different then.

Can you show me the difference? Maybe you can understand at

least a little better now, Jesus' answer to his disciples about the time and seasons being kept from us. The simple answer is we have no capacity to retain or sift out that kind of knowledge.

Didn't God, telling the Jews in the Old Testament about his plan of redemption say, "though a man tell you about it you will not perceive?" Jesus told his disciples "I have many things to tell you but you could not receive it." The truth is, about the things in revelations, the battle of Armageddon, the millennial reign and other things, cannot be put into our times and seasons.

The Bible was not written in chronological order, for multiple reasons, one is he does not have to deal with the devil and his angles from being laid out on a straight line to follow and he can reveal times and seasons to the ones that can hear him, at his will, when necessary. You can see these sleazy tricks anywhere, about any time you are listening to a conversation or anytime you want to tune in on anything going on. Recently when the teacher's union rose up in a big effort to collect $10,000 severance pay for a school teacher that had been convicted of rape and sentenced to go to prison Bill O'Rilley was taking Emails about it. Most people was saying how immoral and wrong they thought it was, this one lady wrote in, "That he paid his union dues and it was their duty to do the best they could for him." Now that sounds very noble and in our society is true and very excepted, but that kind of brings up at least a slate pink flag for me, or maybe blood red, was it not selling God's favoritism the subject for Martin Luther's pulling away from the so called Mother church, some years back? Did not this plant the root for about all the protestant religions? That at first was called reformers. I have been told that Luther never preached dividing the church or pulling away from the church but reforming the church back to what God had said.

How did that work out for everybody? Seems everybody grabs a piece of the pie and goes out to start his own church. Sounds like the same thing that happened at the building of the tower of Babel. When God scattered them out they all seemed to take their own spirit of how to build their own tower. You would have thought maybe one of them would have thought of using God for a tower, or maybe at least a ladder. Many of them that left the mother church rolled a lot of rocks and did very well until man got into control of running it. Man has never taken anything away from God and kept it running well very long, including America.

This description is not just true for the reformation church but basically true for every denomination in it. They dry up the very same way. It looks like God could get one started that he could keep in charge of for a while. Seems most preachers have a problem seeing that God said in his word that his Son was set at the head of the church over all of mankind the only thing between God's wrath and man is Jesus Christ not the government, the government is not to make intercession for us to the church or to God. The church is told to give prayer for the government not as between us and God, only with us.

Everything being what it is according to where you are seeing it at. Look at things from God's point of view. It's the only one that counts. This concept is the very problem of our nation and everybody in it. In throwing out God and denying anything Godly we are leaving ourselves with nothing, so that is exactly what we have. In throwing God out of our colleges, laws, courts, churches, homes and complete society, we've threw out morality, decency, consideration, respect and everything Godly. All we have left is our own inventions and creations, like unions, lawyers, schools, reporters, false religions on every level and every purpose and self-interest, measuring everything by earthly value, money, which is like water, it all belongs to God. (We invented prisons to)

Who is looking out for his interest? All of these things work for money, if you don't have money you don't have anybody looking out for you but yourself and God, and O'Rilley, you know what they have taught us to say, "anyone who goes to court representing himself has a fool for a lawyer," I wonder who taught us that? Probably one of these Christian lawyers that I've been hearing so much about but not from my Bible, it says woe unto you lawyers, now that's what the Bible says, don't pick no fight with me, I'll just let you deal with my big brother, he handles my heavy work. But don't just drop your guard completely I've had to learn a little bit about fighting since I've gotten too old to run.

Our lawyers, like Moses, are trained in all the ways of Pharaoh, paid in accordance to their skill to sell lies, deceit, and any other trick from his bag of skills that he can get away with, even to suppressing truth to help a man to beat the law even if he knows the man is guilty, with no regard to God, Truth or Morality. I thought courts were set up and paid for by tax payers' money in order to find the truth and administer justice and fairness for all, but not so any more, it's sold for money to the highest bidder. It is not the color of the skin that has made the justice system so unjust. I would rather be a black in a white man's court than a white in a black man's court. All the justice you get is what you can pay for. That's how it is when God is thrown out. How low have we sunk? Glad you asked, I'll try to answer that, That lady that retired from the supreme court a short while back, (not a bit too soon), in talking to the press remarked, "Oh I know you cannot legislate morality," I was thinking, how can you legislate without it? That's how low we have sunk. How low and stupid a line can they use to throw out any Godly influence. Answer that and you will know how low they will sink, if God tarries.

I thought God does a pretty good job of legislating morality and has told us how but of course we've out grew him and made him to be foolish and old fashioned. Someone is going to have to call him down here some day and straighten him out. That news lady that thinks Obama, "just might be the smartest man on earth," I'm sure if she could get O'Rilley, Goldburg, Pelosi, Reid to help him, I don't see, with a team like that, how God could possibly have a chance, especially since Sen. Kennedy is already up there to help them, and I'm sure he's already giving God a hard time over them queers, maybe we should send them up there to help him I would not object to see them go if they wanted. Of course that is the reason they want to forget him, they hate him.

God said he would turn into hell any nation and any people who would dare do that, and they don't understand why our nation is headed to hell in a hand basket? A blind man should be able to see that. I marvel at the ignorance of our college trained God hatters, law makers and lawyers using as an excuse for their getting away with it, "were getting paid for doing our best for him," by throwing out all restraint for anything ungodly? Some people will sell their soul for a little pocket change. I know exactly what W. Bush meant when he said, leaving the White House, "well, I didn't sell my soul to them." And I don't believe that he did.

I'm remembering a rabbit trail back a ways that I feel like covering a little. It's about the angels that left their habituate and the only ones I know about, that is now suffering an eternal hell fire. Sounds like the only sin that God felt necessary to judge that harsh that quick and said it's for an example to all of us forever. We know why it was so important, it was going to wreck his plan to develop a perfect bloodline to his son Jesus, he wanted even to develop a perfect blood line from the Jews, and I figure he did. Jesus said salvation was of the Jews.

God knew ever thing about DNA back then, and so many other things that he still has not revealed to us yet, and we won't know until he is ready for us to. He created it all you know, are do you? He gave reproduction to his earthly creation, before then we have no record of it ever existing. Jesus said the angles don't have it. If man could just receive it, creation and this little experiment of God's is, as Joe Biden says a big—deal and we are part of it.

What a privilege and we want to gripe and complain, I'm sure that God wonders about us, and if we are not thankful I believe he is going to let us slide, he has said as much and I believe he means it. It seems to me like the Jews may have been promised perpetual regeneration ability. Jesus talked about worlds to come. The Word talks about the many things God has prepared for them that love him and will live according to his calling and purpose, I cannot see being satisfied with this world down here.

All he asked for us to do is to believe him, and says this creation is enough evidence to convince us, that if we don't believe him we are without excuse, oh man. I'm trying to establish enough grounds to lay a little strong controversial word on. It is about the habituate and purpose God created each of us in, it is laid out very plain in the word where and what each one's place and purpose is, with a few exceptions of a few victims that have fallen to some freaks of nature that only the lord knows why, I'm sure he does.

I'm sure God intends for us to live, learn, grow, and develop in this habitat and to teach our children the same thing. He told his people, under the law, that man with man or man with animal to put them to death. Jesus himself said, he did not come to put the laws away and that not one jot nor tittle will be changed till all things be fulfilled. But the enforcer has been changed, Isaiah said when Jesus comes, the government will be on his shoulders it's not on the Christians they do not have to be their own government any more it worked well under the Egyptians, it worked well under the Babylonians, it worked well under the Romans simply because they would not governor themselves, they would not let judges rule them they would not let the kings God gave them rule them, God scattered them over the world, permitted ever nation on earth to persecute them, then raised up the nation that was best to them in all the world to set his people Israel back into its land. So now we thank were smarter than God. Look at all the nations he used to feed Israel, to punish Israel, to increase Israel, to finance Israel, always some other nation done to and for them what they needed. But when God was through with them nations, or they quit doing things for God the way he wanted them done. God was through with them and it was over for them, God judged them, gave them their reward and they were gone. What I am getting around to saying, we have quit God and he is through with us and we are going down, it's up to us to decide how far and how hard we go, it don't make God a lot of difference, we have had plenty of warning and been given plenty of time to prepare or to repent but we are for the most part already been given over to a reprobate mind, read about it in the 1st chapter of the book of Romans, being given over to a reprobate mind is the last step, I call it the give up of God, they are filled with every evil that can be named, homosexual and sexual perversion of all sorts are the first things named, a man that has decided to be a women, is deciding to leave his God created habitat. I would say so. By blaming God we thank we can be free and do as we please. They feel they would be more pleased to leave their estate and occupy another habituate, God says, them that are just pleased with such things are deserving of death, Romans 1st chapter. I didn't write the Bible I just preach it, even though most people hate it. I cannot help that either, I happened to love it. I have no intention of quitting as long as there is breath in my old body. These that are murmuring and dissatisfied because they cannot be the boss of everything they are involved in are serving the earth's spiritual god, Lucifer, that is riding the white horse of the 6th chapter of Revelations, the red horse following him is the antichrist, the head of Lucifer's army that is riding over the earth with the power of Lucifer and his fallen angles that was dragged out of heaven with the dragon's tail, and will lead the largest army made up from every nation of the earth thinking they can surround the camp of Jesus Christ and his saints at Armageddon, which is the name God gave to the place where the battle is to take place in God's mountains around Jerusalem. This war between God and Lucifer has been going on since before creation I believe. God could have threw him into hell 6,000 years ago, with no trouble, but this is just an example of the patience and long suffering of God that he has told us about.

Lucifer took control of the earth through eve in the garden, It seems like a long time ago to man, 6ooo years to us, but God said it's like 6 days to him. He don't see time as we do, it has no limits to him. We can put no limits on him in time, space, distance, or anything else, I suppose there might be something somewhere that he could be measured with but it sure is not in our creation. This is why Jesus said it's not for you to know the times and the seasons that the father has reserve unto himself, I've always said God could give you a thousand years, give me 5 years and make them end at the same time if he wanted, we would never know how he done it even if he told us we are not equipped to receive it, so why would we want to worry about it, again whatever God says is good enough for me, I really don't have time to argue with him. (I'd say that's bold talk for a one eyed fat man.) To think man can put God into a time frame of man's size would be just plain foolishness, if you lay down tonight and wake up in the morning to still be breathing you need to be thankful to God for it will not be that way forever, only a fool would think it will be. He says to give thanks in and for everything.

God says the flesh is at war with the spirit, the Bible tells of the battles all up through it from the beginning of time, the kingdoms of Egypt, Assyrian, Babylon, Medes Persia, Grecians, then

Rome down to the split into the two legs, with the feet, Middle Eastern kingdoms and the West kingdoms of today, consisting of the gentile kingdoms with Gog and Magog consisting of wars and rumors of wars, nation against nation, kingdom against kingdom, famines, pestilence, and earthquakes, these are the beginnings of sorrows, brother killing brother.

Then comes the ten end time kingdoms, I call them, that are raising in and around the old roman empire, they are raising right now and will rule the world as the western kingdoms will be completely losing their dominion, but their lives will be spared, the ten kingdoms will rule the world and make a 7yr. treaty with Israel but 42 mo. is as long as it will last. The ten toes will burn that great city, the whore that has corrupted ever religion and kingdom on the earth, and has ruled over kings on the earth, from over the face of the earth. While the rich merchants of the earth watch the smoke of her burning and mourn in amazement. Then a king will rise up out of one of the ten kingdoms, will rip three of the other kingdoms up by the roots and the others will give their kingdoms to him and Lucifer, or any one of the dozen or so names he has been given, that has been battling God since the creation, he will give all his power to the red horse rider, after the 1ooo year reign and he has been released from prison he will organize the nations of the world and will surround the camp of Jesus Christ and his saints at Jerusalem for the last big battle for Lucifer to try to take over the entire works.

I have been trying to confess and explain about the times and the seasons of these last happenings, I do not know the sequence of these events Jesus said they were not given to us and this is what he was talking about. But I believe everything I said is going to happen for it is written in God's word, and I believe it is neigh at hand for so many of these things are happening I'm convinced the ball is done been started to roll. We have been told that it will be picking up speed, rolling faster and faster.

There is another point I'd like to make, Solomon said there is nothing new under the sun so I don't even believe in preaching something new until the end has come. Then Jesus said he was going to make all things new but that is another sermon. I'm trying to come back a little closer to where we are at, now I have talked a lot about wars, Lucifer has been warring with God since creation, flesh warring against the spirit, Christians warring against the world, if Obama knows two people he is trying to pit them against one another in as much war as he can get going. I just about don't know nothing or anybody that is free of war. So wars is nothing new, God and Lucifer have been battling through all the history he has given us, of course God has never lost a battle but Lucifer would probably say that he hasn't either, and I would guess God could give you a few thousand reason for ever battle, one is he is going to set down at a supper table with a saved Israel and a table full with tested and proven children that he is going to have a good reason to be proud of ever one of them and many more reasons for everything I'm sure.

I can just picture Lucifer building up his pride and confidence thanking maybe that God hadn't been able to polish him off yet, I have done some reading and in my pondering on this I come up with a few things, I noticed out of all the battles I could not find where Jesus and Lucifer has ever come face to face in a confrontation until he surrounds Jesus and the saints with the fullest intent of finishing them off completely. That is going to be the biggest and shortest battle and I hope the last battle on record and it will be the end of Lucifer, as he will be cast alive into a lake of fire. Lesson here is, or as they used to say when our parents would finish an interesting story that was simple enough for us to understand, like the "three little pigs," or "the three bears," or "wolf, wolf," the moral to the story is;.., But what they would not teach without, has become foolishness to our smart teachers of today, and why not since we have made moral itself to be a foolish thing that cannot be legislated or taught by our government. And it was outlawed for other institutions in public. The Bible says, "without parables, Jesus taught them not," but our government has made Jesus look so stupid his name is not permitted to be spoken in any school activity, a very dangerous man, our kids are taught. Have you got the gall to tell me that this does not bother you and you're a Christian? I hope you can convince Jesus Christ, you can't convince me, for sure, but Jesus is the only one you have to convince, not me, but Jesus did say I could know them by their fruits. Do you want to look with me at the fruits of our schools and our government and defend them to me? You may have the gall to try to defend your being a Christian but I cannot imagine someone dumb enough to except the second challenge.

Like I mumble to the Lord about every time I pray, which I try to do all the time, Lord, I believe maybe the hardest assignment you can hand out to a man is to get out truth to a people that don't want it, and they hate it. It sure gives me a lot more respect for God's prophets than I used to have with just half the understanding as I have now, and am sure I could use a lot more of understanding, but am not so sure how much of it I can stand or handle.

When I get to feeling to sorry for myself I look at Glenn Beck, I feel every attack that man gets and it makes me feel better about my problems. He's my man and I've knew it from about the second or third time I saw him on TV away back there, I thought how in the world did that man ever get on that TV station? He stood out like a black at a KKK meeting, in Mississippi. As I've already stated somewhere else in this, by their own records, over half of the ones they hung, were white, but all of them where Republicans. Democrats still refer to the Republicans today as the enemy, and terrorist, but you are not allowed to call such people that bombs our very country, kills our solders, declared war on us, sworn to cleans the earth of Christians and Jews, bombs our social events, I could go on but surely that is enough to get my point across, we cannot call these people the same names as they call Republicans, these people are their friends they are on their payroll and you will be charged with a hate crime and given a long prison sentence if you as much as hurt their feelings.

But Republicans are these names and everybody is given open season on them, not just their enemy but THE enemy. I've heard them say so. And we cannot tell the spiritual side they are on? Jesus Christ the spirit of God, or Lucifer the spiritual god of this world? remember Jesus said you are either gathering with us are you are scattering abroad, take your choice you will only have to meet your own record, nobody else, and you will get it, and you will be judged by the spiritual side you have aligned your spirit with. Jesus or Lucifer, everything in twos, one side or the other, God says a man that cannot control his own spirit is like a city with its walls tore down.

If you're like most of us you'll know more about everybody else's record than you'll know about your own. That not only will not help you, but it will not hurt anybody else either. If that is the sum of what you take into judgment with you don't expect to make a very big splash when you land there, and you will land there. If I was a smart person maybe I could write them a sad song that might help them out. I have written a few. Stay tuned for the next chapter.

CHAPTER 13

Singing and Making Melody to the Lord

There are things I'd like to bring in here that I have observed, and would like to bring in about singing, to roll it around a little to help our understanding, judgment, receiving and giving and hopefully a lot of other things.

Music is made by tones, set in an order to make a sound that is considered to be pleasing to the ones who hears and considers it pleasant and pleasing to them. Much is to be said about a person, considering the kind of music he likes and listens to and enjoys.

Like words themselves they are judged to be what they are by the spirit they were spoken from, and what spirit that received them was of. The antichrist spirit hates, and is offended with any musical sound or song that gives glory to God. Many of us cannot tell the difference between the carnal spirit and the spirit of God so the only way to judge anything about the situation is the appearance of the situation, now I admit that is a very revealing way, usually reveals very much, so why did Jesus say to not judge by the appearance of a thing? I suppose we're expected to just dismiss it like everything else Jesus said. That's what our government teaches us to do. After all he's a stupid radical you know, and so dangers to our children till we are not allowed by our laws to mention his name in the schoolhouse our to allow a cross to be seen on a public place that our government has invested a dime in, at any time.

That is like fooling with a loaded gun, the government better be called in on that, with a swat team with all precaution. So if you have a local school teacher, and you hear they used the name Jesus Christ in front of your defenseless child, or in hearing distance thereof you should call your ACLU immediately or you may be arrested for being a negligent parent. If you can't get things going by your glorious ACLU, which I figure you can, but if not, your chances are good your congressman will be an active member of that brave upstanding organization of dedicated men and women, determined to keeping you and your children completely safe by separating our government and state from the name of that stupid, lying, dangerous man, The Lord Jesus Christ.

Don't worry about support if you can just get this outlaw school teacher to court we have thousands and thousands of judges ready to beat her about the head and ears severally with their gavel and make her replace the gavel for them in the court cost, and don't forget to ask for restitution, we have a tremendous judicial system in this country it will prosecute and impeach a state's highest judge for displaying the ten commands. When I mentioned it amidst a few preachers right after it happened, one of the pasture preachers jumped right up with, "now Bro. Bill you know the Bible tells us we have to obey the laws of the land" I still have not found out what kind of a bible they had been reading from, but it's not the same Bible I carry, and we have preachers like that, pasturing our churches under the name of Jesus Christ, they should not hate that Jesus, it's just the name that they hate and anything they can tie to it. They do not know the spirit of God, or cannot recognize anything by the righteous spirit, only by appearance and what somebody told them. And we wonder where the problem is? I guess we should be like everybody else, it's God fault, he told me to say it. But that should tell us a little why Jesus said not to judge by appearance but judge a righteous judgment, so when you judge anything you better know something about the Word of God which is Jesus Christ, which is righteous, and has already judged everything. If you don't, just put your trust in God and let him do the judging, I'm sure he can handle it.

Only the word of God is sharp enough to separate the joints and the morrow and I'm certain it is able to separate even in the middle of a song what parts give glory to the carnal ego, and the parts that give glory to the spirit of God. It's our minds that get confused, not the Spirit of God or the Word of God. We often throw out the baby with the bath water if you know what I mean.

I'll give you a small example. Look for the point, not too much at the details, for the point can be applied to a multiple of different situation. Early in my living for God, experiences, one of my very early pastures, a great man of God for many years around close to 40 years ago, at the time, of whom I learned so many things from and thank God constantly for ever being allowed to cross paths with him in this life, and feel like I owe him so very much. He was of the old class and held onto a lot of hard core beliefs, some of them to a fault maybe. He was preaching one time and was coming down very hard on country music. Well I say kind of fondly, I raised myself on country music and very well know that you can preach all day on evils in and of country music, especially what it has become today, but let us look at it a little closer since we all think that we are the perfect judge on anything and everything. This preacher getting down on these people, of course having them into a bunch, depicted them into a scene and saying, they would sing that filthy stuff for so long, then after a while they would slow everything down and announce it was time to do a hymn, they would take off their big hats, gather around the mike and sang a gospel song, insinuating very heavy like they were mocking God, poking fun at them or him I'm not real sure, but obviously at how sorry he thought they were. I was setting there thinking how thankful and happy I was that these very talented, legendary and great singers and musicians would take the time to give God some recognition in their show, depending on where you are looking at it from, I guess.

But I refuse to believe that God was offended at them giving a little time, glory, praise, and honor to the all mighty God and creator of this whole creation. It almost made me want to cry just to hear him tell about it. I wondered if he could give a little room for somebody else's opinion about it? Opinions are free you know. Hank Williams wrote and sang so many religious songs maybe unequaled, I don't know, how about, "when the fire comes down from heaven," or "from Jerusalem to Jericho," "when the pale horse and his rider goes by." I could fill this page with tittles alone and some of the songs make as good a sermon as I've heard preached from a pulpit. Just oweing to the spirit you are of, I preach any way. When Hank died his mother said that his songs would live as long as people lived and fell in love and died. That seems to be right so far.

Ferlin Husky sang that country music was from the heart and that it was here to stay, common sense in other words and God is the author of common sense, and from the heart, the heart being the part of us where God looks at. I've read the part where God recorded the song of Moses, may be on record as the first song ever recorded, I don't know. One of the books of the Bible is called the Song of Solomon. David was sent to sang songs and play his harp for Saul and drive the evil spirits away from the king of Israel. I wonder if he would have sung rap or rock and roll of our time if it would have drove the evil spirits away.

The book of Psalms consist mostly of the songs of David, seems they are all about glorying God and when David danced in front of the ark, knowing David, I would about bet a pretty penny that he was singing a little bit, but maybe we will never know.

All of these things assures me that an evil spirit hates, and may not can even stand, singing that praising God. That is why the evil spirits that run this world has everybody of this world attacking any song or any singer that has as much as a religious sound to it. Ricky Skaggs almost lost his recording contract for mixing too much of his faith in God in his tour's testimony. Just for giving glory to the God that created him and had performed miracles through answered prayer.

And here is my pastor attacking all of country music and sending to hell anybody who would sang it. I've had many others to attack me worse than that. I don't have time and space to tell about them all, you would not want to hear them anyway. I just want to make a few points. One of them is, man is a poor judge to be judging anything but sometimes we have to, but when we don't have to, I can promise you that most of the time it will be better off left alone, and if he don't know the spirit of something then he just don't know it, even if he knows the spirit of something that don't mean he knows all about it, but it does mean he knows something. When the other way probably what he thinks he knows is likely wrong.

I just pray God will look on me half as well as I know he is going to look upon Hank Williams when we all get to judgment. That is why when I was kind of arguing with God about preaching. I told him, among other things, that if he expected me to get out there and try to please man or if man was going to be there to judge me when I get through, that he could just forget about me because I had more sense than to tackle either one of them projects. I knew I could never make a good Liberal.

God spoke to me very promptly and said that I would not ever be called on to judge a man and there would never be a man set between him and me in judgment. I am very thrilled until today for that promise for it is much more real and plainer now than it was around 40 years ago. I held no ill feeling toward that pastor and never confronted him in any way about it, but I believe I saw him missing blessing for such similar mistakes, that's my opinion.

As we have said, the Bible is full of battles from the beginning of time up until now, the reason being Lucifer started a rebellion that has spread all through heaven and earth seems like everything God creates falls right into it, now God could destroy it and him instantly but he is full of pity, mercy and patience he will not do it that way, but he has seen long ago that he is going to have to destroy this creation and start over with it.

It is no problem with him but will be disastrous to anybody who hates righteousness, despises any kind of control even if it is a perfect, all righteous control with great reward, we had rather join Lucifer who fills our independent ego and lustful desire to be below nobody in nothing, with nothing but lies and false accusations against anything true. With, it won't be this way if we can just kill Jesus.

Well they did but it did not help anything that I ever read about, but brought total disaster on the ones that did it. Having to have someone to blame, (sounds like the democrats, don't it? it is), so they say, well it's his influence, we've got to kill his influence.

Reminds me of a piece of writing that was supposed to have come from some of France's records that one of Napoleon Bonaparte's associates was talking to him about some people problems, and he asked Napoleon if he believed that Jesus was still alive.

He supposedly walked over to a window looking out over a busy street from a higher window, for a solemn minute or so, turned back around and said something like, "I know of a lot of men that have come and gone, no man dead could have this kind of influence on people, yes, he is alive," so after 2000 years they are still trying to kill his influence on people, you'd think they would give up, after 2000 years, but God has said there will always be a few remaining and they will be preaching the everlasting gospel of peace, and always be hated and persecuted by the world.

The wars between Jesus Christ, that wants and gives nothing but peace, and the devil who wants and has no purpose but to kill, steal and destroy, has always went on, and will always go on until Jesus comes back and totally destroys the devil and anybody that has been deceived by him and believes his lies and chooses to align with him and fight against truth and to kill, steal and destroy anything attached to truth.

For the life of me I cannot understand why anybody cannot see and tell the difference in the spirit of the two and would not want to choose the spirit of truth to fight on its side when self and flesh is the only enemy they have to defeat.

The Babylonian beast, starting with the head of solid gold in Daniel, is the same beast saw by John in the book of revelations, just changes heads down to the split off like a man's legs, the East and the West sides of the earth today, the wealth, power and gospel developed the West Side to set God's people back in their land and to preach the gospel to the world and then will come the end. We are living in the times of the feet now, times of the beginning of sorrows, wars and rumors of wars, so wars aren't letting up, they are just getting started, and god's people, mostly Jews, with a few grafted in gentiles, are coming into times like there has never been before on this earth and will never be again. So if you have been hearing preaching about the rapture, and the end time revival that is going to fill the churches with a shouting rejoicing people before the coming of the Lord, and many more false illuminations that is contrary to anything I have read in my whole Bible. I can give you about a few dozen scriptures that tells you the exact opposite of what they are preaching, maybe you can suggest to them to read a little in the word of God.

Rapture is one of the things that the great whore, rider of the beast of Daniel and Revelations, mother of harlots and abominations of the earth, drunk on the blood of the saints, never been given the name of a beast even though she ruled over kings on the earth, but a rider of beast that come and go but she remains a whore and rider of the beast. She was the organizer of the rapture theory centuries ago, now seems about all the churches are starting to think it is a beautiful sounding story, just too beautiful to resist, and no telling how many books have been sold telling it.

But the ten kingdoms that are rising up in the East leg of the Roman kingdom that God has said would rise up and rule the world and produce the Antichrist, that the devil is going to give all his power to at one time and season, will eat the flesh of the whore and will burn her with fire, The beginning of sorrows and times and seasons like never been that we cannot put in order for it has not been given unto us, but we know it's coming and it will consist of mostly the East fighting against the West. The West will lose and then the northern kingdom will meet the kingdom of the south in the mountains around Jerusalem, and these will be the times and seasons that we cannot put in any order to us, and no flesh would be spared if God did not intervene, everybody will be losers and bloodshed will have never had an equal. The Christians will not have a side to get on but God's side and it will be hated by both side and God is busy pouring out the tribulations and wrath, the tabernacle in heaven will be filled with smoke and no man can enter into it. God says anything that can be shaken will be shaken at one time he says blessed is he that dies in the Lord from this time on.

Men will seek death but death will flee from them, many things more God does say, it's all in the Bible. Now you're thinking, that cannot be so, for we bore the labor through the heat of the day and God will not allow me to stay here through the end time heat and receive the same pay as the ones that just get in on the end of the day, he is going to rapture me out of here before any trouble.

In the parable Jesus told these complainers that they were paid what they agreed to work for, so they had no grip coming, and the paying was his job and it was none of their business what or how he paid somebody else. He told Peter about the same thing when he asked what he was going to do with John, Jesus replied to Peter that it did not concerned him in no way at all.

We will be rewarded by and for our works, but salvation is the same for everybody and it will all be up to Jesus to judge both and I'm sure he don't need our help or advice and he has made it very plain he does not like grumblers or complainers. Maybe we should examine where we are at on any issue, Jesus says to just follow him. I figure that is good advice.

If you look through any or all of these battles told about up through God's word you will notice one single factor missing in every single battle in every single war, Lucifer has never tangled with Jesus, the Son of God, Jesus out of his love and mercy has not allowed the world, Satan, Lucifer, mankind or anything else entangle him. He even told them at the cross, you are not taking my life, I'm laying it down, I have the power to lay it down and to pick it up again. And told them from off the cross, know you not that I could pray the father and have12 leagues of angles presently here. If one angle can selectively kill 85,000 Syrians in one night, and as I add to it, and didn't even raise a sweat, can you imagine what 12 leagues of angles could do? No you can't.

This is the difference in all of these wars, they have never tangled with Jesus Christ, until Armageddon, he's a devil whipper ever time, God tells of the results I suppose in a dozen places or so and it's not a pretty site either. And if he only has two saints with him in his camp the results is going to be the same. These denominations that have refused to accept a bloody salvation from Jesus Christ's blood will sacrifice their own blood to the other god from heaven, Lucifer, and will spend eternity with him in hell. I do not know of another way to tell you about it. Jesus is riding the White horse of revelations 19th chapter, which is dedicated entirely to Jesus Christ dressed for and already engaged in the last battle before the one thousand year reign, called the millennial rein, and the beginning of the battle of Armageddon, which looks like to me a very short battle, read the 14th, chapter of Isaiah see the release of Satan after the thousand year reign and read about the finishing up of the battle of Armageddon. I cannot see any question of who the winner is or how completely the victory is going to be in the end.

Think God for his mercy and put your complete trust in him and endure until the end. Your flesh cannot but your soul and spirit can if aligned with the Spirit of God like he said, which is the only way. Our complete problem is that we worry too much about our fleshly side and cannot embrace our own soul and spiritual side, face it, you are not going to save your fleshly side, it's already dead to God, turn it loose. It has been given, now seventy years owing to the way we take care of it, but it is a wonderful ride and ever spirit is envious toward us and wants to occupy one of these bodies, but God chose it for you, and if you can love righteous living and willing to be subject to him and prove it, he is willing to give you a new glorious body, elevated above his angles, one with his son, and be there throughout eternity.

The prophets and the disciples and the rest of us that can become the children of Abraham and can inherit his vision and can walk in it, has this promise, most of them died for it. How much of it do you think they would have accomplished if they would have accounted their old fleshly bodies and self-interest first, and before the spiritual side that is God that created it all. Not only is it the only way to endure to the end, it's the only way for anything to do so. This is what God's word meant when he said all things are predestinated, you read your Bible you can see where all things are predestinated for the end of all things are foretold by what chose they want to choose, or what road they want to walk down. The end of that road is described in the Word of God until we are without excuse for taking the wrong road.

The Word of God is our guide and a lamp to our feet. Can't you see by now why are government hates it so much as to form a Comity of separation of Jesus and government for he exposes all the lying, hypocritical, evil surmising which is all they consist of if you add a little selfishness, hate, greed, envy, strife, and fraud. I could think of at least a dozen more words that would fit into this list very well but I would not want to burn you out with too many in one place. Maybe I could suggest to them they should burn the cross out in California that is so terribly offensive to them. That is what the southern Democrats did in the hay days of the KKK when they were hanging Republicans and getting away with it.

The Democrats, like all other evils are pushing it off on the Republicans like they were the ones hanging themselves all along. And the people being reprobates and craving a good sounding lie were much more than just anxious to believe it. Any lying power grabber has to have a scape goat. The Democrats know they have to keep enough Republicans elected for a scape goat, especially since they almost threw out too many Republicans at the end of the bush administration in order to get the president's office back, it got so one sided they had a little trouble blaming the Obama health care plan on them, even tried to deny it was named after Obama, tried to say it was Romney's health care plan. Caused a lot of ignorant people I know to not go to vote at all, Hard to criticize Democrats when they have it working so well for themselves but it don't speak to well for the intelligence of the voters, but them being happy enough with him to do it again maybe it's my mind that slipped the track, one of us has for sure.

The Democrats were able to convince the Blacks, along with most of the rest of the world that it was the Republicans that was hanging the Negros that they had just finished fighting and won the war for their freedom for them. That doesn't make good sense in my mind so it must be my mind that is off track for sure. I believe it's like everything else I've been talking about, it depends on the direction you are looking at it from, or the direction from which your receiving it from and the ones that are being benefited by it.

If we cannot come together on them we will never come into agreement, and then if we cannot come to see it together from God's position we are both wrong still. Now you should be able to see why the world is in such terrible shape, then you need to look at how and what they benefited, was it carnal or spiritual, then you will know which one they are serving, follow the money as they say. Then look into God's word, you can study it and see their end reward and where they are headed. Fairly well informed I'd say.

That is why God said to study and meditate on his word, you can be informed and preach and teach wisdom to them that hear but your still not qualified to judge anybody but yourself. That is God's department and you can depend on him to do it, just follow him is what he says. I'm kind of trimming down on letting the devil and God hating people into my life and home but not in my church. I've always said the devil himself can set on the front pew as long as he don't get interruptive, but he will have to sit on a hot seat and listen to the word of God, I find most of them cannot stand very much of it, for very long. I have had them to leave the church in a number of strange ways but I have never had to ask anyone to leave my church.

One of them left after throwing his coffee cup against the wall and stomped out the door mumbling a few obscenities with nobody from the church helping him at all. Of course he started making phone calls and attacking the church people including myself, he was smart enough to call the worst enemy in this country against the Christian church, the government officials, E.P.A, Home Health, Family Planning, and all such. I believe he has all their numbers in his pocket. He was known by us to have pulled this trick against people and businesses that he didn't like across three states for years, that he was often bragging about what he cost them. He caused us a little trouble for the government is always more than ready to start any investigation on about anybody that there might be a chance to promote their job, and that means a small preacher is at the head of the list for he has got all the rich and famous people that he has not given favoritism too and over half of any other group of people all ready to believe anything against him because a preacher is supposed to be faultless. People that read this are already figuring on things wrong with me in what I've said here, have a field day, ok? So the law and investigators are always more than ready to exercise their authority and presenting their threats, of course they are not interested in nothing but your safety. If you don't believe me, just ask them. Have not I already mentioned that authority is among the #1 lusted after words of all, I know most people would probably say money or sex, but if you had enough authority you could get all the other you can handle. I believe most of the People I was talking about seem to get just about as much thrill out of authority as they do out of any of the other things. I would not know, It's leaning a little toward the judging department which I say belongs to God, but he says we should judge a righteous judgment, and I was only stating things as facts as I saw them not as I would judge them.

It will all be judged and rewarded in the final judgment, which most people call the white throne judgment which God has told us some about but not much in detail, mostly about the setting and the purpose, and the results. God says the purpose is to call up all the dead from everywhere including graves, hell, and the seas, to be rewarded for their works. As far as I can read this judgment is all about works, each and every one will receive their reward for their works, whether good or bad. God says we will be paid.

That is one reason they will be called from everywhere, no one will be missed. I had an Assembly of God preacher tell me that we would all receive the same pay, the ones that were saved would receive heaven, and the ones that were not would receive hell, each one being the same reward. His reason given, was the parable of the penny a day proved that we would all receive the same pay. If that was so I could throw half of my bible away as being useless, so I choose to just stay with God's word and believe what he says. Talk about wresting the scriptures with ignorance, I believe that one would about take the #1 cake. The results God gives us, is everybody will be rewarded for their works.

Death and hell along with them whose names were not found written in the Lambs book of life would be cast into the lake of fire. Here is where a lot of our knowledge just plainly stops, who can know just whose names are written in the book of life.

I believe it is called the Lamb's book, I have not been told of nobody who has been given a peep at it so that leaves open every man's opinion to discussion, with very little to discuss it with or over, except opinions. God's judgment is very lightly explained when it comes to details, as most of the things of God is, I think I have explained why, mostly we do not have the capacity to receive, retain or understand it correctly.

When it is about somebody else, he told peter it was none of his business. I do not know anything about these things more than what the Bible affirms, but I'm sure some preachers think they know all about God's judgment, knows about the white throne judgment, the lake of fire, the rapture and times of the beginning, and the times of the end, the lambs book of life, the names that are in it and the names that are out of it. I just have not reached that level yet, I'm still studying and seeking, don't give up on me yet. So let Bill O' and his sidekick Goldburg set up there on tv and tell how smart they are and where they went to school and how much education they have, how many books they have wrote and read and how smart their authors are and how big a name they have attained. Then say such things like, "you cannot go to the Bible for truth after all it condones slavery," is slavery a lie? Goldburg said, "some people believe the world is just 6000 yrs. Old" but, "he didn't care if Jesus Christ and God both said the earth was just 6000 years old it was just not so, the earth was 4.8 billion years old and that was a fact." O'Rilley said, "the things Jesus told about happing, just could not have happened, and he could prove it." I was thinking if I ever talk to them I believe I will tell them that I do not believe that either one of them was born to their mothers, that a long legged, long beaked, long winged stork delivered them, wrapped in a towel and set them on her front porch, see if they could prove me wrong.

I'd like to see the proof they could show me, their talk sounds like, mighty bold talk for a one eyed fat man, and their one eye must be crossed or maybe blind like Jesus said it is. The god of this world has blinded their minds so the light of the glorious gospel cannot shine into their hearts so Jesus might save them. They are trying to set God into a time frame so they can crucify him again. All two of them with a world full of demon processed, God hating people trying to help them can never convince one of God's people that will just fully believe the word of God, there is any truth in their philosophy. Of course God's word says in the last days everything that can be shaken will be shaken, I prefer to be one of them that cannot be shaken off. Just keep believing and endure until the end and be saved. All of them that receives the spirit of the god of this world, his name, mark or the #of a man will be shook off and will worship the antichrist and will burn up with the fire that will burn up this world that they so foolishly chose.

If we choose to walk in the spirit of God the creator, in faith, and in hope we will be hated by the world, persecuted by the wicked that lay in wait constantly for a chance to slay anybody called righteous. Which side are you on?

If you are a Christian you will definitely be standing out and be seen by all. The Bible says it will not be hard to tell the ones that are God's they will be minding the things of the spirit. If of the world they will be minding the things of the flesh. God has created man and this galaxy in a short time zone, each man's time here is like a puff of smoke, here today gone tomorrow, what makes man think that he will be able to move into God's seat and take control of God and put him into man's time zone that he made and gave to us in the first place and gave us a little space in his world and compares our little world to the dust of his feet and we know nothing about the spirit of God and we are going to lower him down to the level of a four footed beast and creeping things and treat him like he is smaller than us? When he is taller than the stars, the havens and earth cannot contain him. Somebody is out of their ever-loving pea brain minds and I don't believe it is God. Man thinks he knows more about God than he knows about himself even back before he created this world, and man to take charge of it, tend and enjoy it. I'm sure he hoped that man would appreciate it and keeps things in their prospective places, especially God himself. If we could keep him in his place the rest would fall in right. Man is selfish, greedy, egotistical and stupid he thinks he can get control of God's seat and kill God's influence and take control of God himself.

The plan came from Lucifer himself, kill his son, the heir, and take over the whole farm. When the plan started, in the 6th chapter of Genesis God cut the years of a man on this Earth and declared that his spirit would not always strive with man, Jesus intervened because he loved man, and his world so much, he made a plan and volunteered to pay the price and promised he could except and save a few, even if it be just a few he would except them as his brotheren and promised that God, his father would except them as his children. What a plan. What a sacrifice. What a love. It cannot be bought with money nor works are anything namable but with genuine love of the Lord Jesus Christ only, the one that God, the father, turned everything on heaven and earth over to. So you are not even dealing with God but with Jesus Christ his son, which is not only a good break for us but the only break we have. If we could go around Jesus and walk into the presents of God we would be instantly consumed without an announcement. God already announced that it had repented him that he had ever made flesh in the first place and the end of all of it had come up before him, it was Jesus that led the children of Israel through the wilderness and with the help of Moses kept the wrath of God off of them, and did so until after the resurrection when Jesus came back and announced to the apostles, and to the world, I've been given all power on heaven and Earth.

The heaven and earth God created through his son, Jesus Christ. Not God's dwelling place. Do you think he just lightly breathed that out or maybe just kind of day dreamed it along or something of that nature, I wish to assure you there is no such writing in the Word of

God, that is the big difference in The Word and any other writing on this earth. There are no misprints in God's word.

Back to Jesus being the mediator between us and the father, do you think it was Jesus, or God that killed Aaron's sons? Who do you think it was that slayed one of David's mighty men for slapping his hand on the ark to steady it when the ox had stumbled? Who do you think it was that jumped on Moses' case? When he struck the rock the second time when God had told him to speak to it, so he did not get to lead his people into the promise land. I don't believe it was Jesus for he was the rock that Moses struck.

I would have seriously objected to this kind of teaching not very long ago but can see a lot clearer and farther now than I could then, I would have saw it as that spirit I have been working against a long time that is trying to separate God and Jesus, this is a dangerous spirit and on a hard mission because it cannot be done, only in some people's minds that are not to stable to start with. But I have been convinced that there is nothing wrong with identifying them, not separating them, Jesus said the Father is greater than I am and did not consider it as a separation.

As I have been saying a word or words only mean what they mean by what the spirit they are of, giving and receiving agrees on. If a spirit that is not contrary to God, starts to align with a spirit that is contrary to God, is it not flirting with the danger of falling? I think it is. God speaks of a people that will not endure sound doctrine, reckon that may be a little of what he was talking about.

That spirit that is contrary to God is the same one that wants to kill the heir and inherit the farm. Can you imagine how foolish that sounds to God? A canal mind cannot. Since O'Rilley and Goldburg know so much about the beginning maybe they can tell us about the end of our time.

They have a lot of preachers, teachers and book writers that are trying to help them, they are good mouth pieces, teaching such things as a rapture, or their denomination is the only one that is going to be saved, once saved always saved, reckon why Jesus told us to endure until the end to be saved?

Things about how, when and where they are going to happen I am dumb myself. I only know what God has told us in his word and some things he has showed me in dreams, visions and revelations which I can only except as God reveals them to me out of his word. I will not try to wrest the scriptures to fit my own beliefs for God says if we wrest scriptures we wrest them to our own destruction, I do not want to do that. I will try not to warp my weak mind with false prophets and teachings, of which the world is overly blessed with and it's not hard to find a preacher that will try to preach these things you want to hear, especially if you will pay him well, I believe Jesus called them hirelings, shake a little money, they're not hard to find, but don't depend to heavy on them when the wolf comes or the money runs low.

I will just take God at his word and hang onto that instead of teachings that gender more questions, strife and confusion than clear answers, like God gives. If we would have had an ancient philosopher writing in his own name, no claim to God, that could claim just 5% of the accurate prophecies as the Bible itself has plainly to its credit, the whole world would be worshiping him till today instead of working so hard to disprove and deny him and trying to disgrace him and to prove him a fake, liar, never existed. I have a hard time understanding mankind and the hatred he has built up for the Lord Jesus for no reason I can see.

One of the reasons I'm a Christian today, I was reading in my Bible and could clearly see I was reading about a man that stood on a mountain side, with a rock behind him for an amplifier and telling multitudes all about my time today, and that was 2000 years ago. That was very impressive to me, got my attention, and the farther I looked into it the more impressive it became. I'm like Pontius Pilate, I find no fault in this man. We have nothing that he did not give us, including the dirt bag we live in

From the teaching of the Bible, we have no right to approach him except lawfully, humbly, and began with thanksgiving. This is why Jesus said to deny the flesh before you come to me. The flesh cannot do these things so it must be dead and reborn into the spirit of God then we, or it, must learn to walk in the spirit.

In grade school I was taught that I could not learn anybody anything, nor could anybody learn me anything. The key being all we can do is teach, the other has to do the learning for themselves. I don't remember if I learned any other intelligent thing in grade school or not but I learned that one, and it is a very intelligent fact and principle. Good enough for God to use on himself, all he can do is teach us we have to do the learning. It is up to us if we choose to learn his ways or not.

How can we learn if we cannot hear? Jesus said my people know my voice and another they will not follow. I've heard that fact claimed as a big weapon and great promise to themselves no it's just a fact that narrowed Jesus' flock of sheep down to a very small number. When you look at it from God's position, which is from the other side of the carnal side of the situation. You can verify that with almost any situation in the entire Bible if you will study on and consider it. The carnal does not hear Jesus' voice. The spirit of God draws our spirit, our spirit must draw our flesh.

With God being up from us any place we are at, if we point to him from any place on the face of the earth we point up, even though we point to the opposite direction than the man in china is pointing, these figures are according to all of our -ologist's facts, which I don't hold much stock in, surely not to hold it above or in front of God's knowledge especially after God has said he put all of man's knowledge below the foolishness of God's knowledge.

Reminds me of a young fireball type preacher getting started out, when a heckler ask him if he really believed that a whale swallowed up Jonah? The young preacher replied, "I sure do". If my Bible would have said that Jonah swallowed up the whale, I would believe that too. God's direction is a little different from ours and I'm completely persuaded that God is the most correct of the two.

When we talk of something being between us and God it seems were usually thinking of it as being in the front of us. I believe God may be thinking a little more of it being above us, hence, if were trying to hand something to God from this carnal earth we must hand it through all the foolishness of God to get it through to him.

Do you really think God wants it after it has been defiled if a carnal thing touches it and it is unclean it will be consumed in his presents? Be careful what we speak to God. This is where the mediator, Jesus, comes in. Can God help it if he is Holy, Righteous, perfect and always knows everything and cannot lie?

Do you expect him to lower himself down to our level, the level of a four footed beast and be judged by man, like about ever man you meet wants to do. Talk to them, they will let you know all about their intentions and their opinions. We have a right to our opinions but I have a lot of opinions about opinions, one of them is they are like noses, everybody has one and is usually willing to push it into anywhere there is an open door, making them one of the cheapest things I know of. You can stop on any busy street corner and in a short while you can pick up all you can carry, and probably not cost you a dime. Not worth much, huh? You could ask a dozen people the same question and it's doubtful if two will give you the same opinion.

That is what puts the value to them, verity, you have the option to pick, even a part of any opinion you have time to listen to. You will probably run out of time before they run out of opinions. Let me try to get this back on communications for it seems to be the root of ever relationship and what I started this book about and trying to build on communication with God because he is the head of everything and is holding the records of all communication.

The government could not carry a candle for God when it comes to spying and keeping records it is no problem for him to know the days doings of 7 billion people a day and not to miss one thing, and man thinks he can compete with that, it's kind of like a chigger crawling up an elephant's leg with rape on his mind. I don't think his opinion will make a very big uproar, but to see things from God's position is just about the only thing that matters. It's facts like this is why God said we should meditate on his word day and night, whether you can see it or not it is the only sound communication root in our entire creation, called truth, and Jesus is the way the truth and the light and life and our only communication to the father, You cannot hardly get an educated preacher that will make that kind of statement, might offend to many different religions. So what, Jesus said in some things we offend them all, he added woe unto them through which the offence comes, not necessarily to the one that did the offending.

Most people you try to talk to will interrupt you in almost any subject you talk on and tell their story about the same happening to them and get it ahead of yours and bigger, or start asking questions as to who it was, or when and where it was, anything but looking to get the point you are trying to make. The trouble is they try to do God the same way, and Jesus' parables the same way.

That kind of communications is only good for curiosity and gossip and to accuse and tear down or to use for their own profit. Or to let you know they are ahead of you and they know more about it than you, and never get the moral, or the point as I call it.

I've heard, so called, big time preachers and writers discussing and even arguing a little over certain ones of Jesus' parables if they were just allegory or really a fact. What difference would it make? If Jesus said it happened I'm not going to tell him he is lying. I do not have the nerve of O'Rilley and Goldburg, I'd not only be scared but I would feel much like a fool.

Similarly when you have somebody working for you, and being paid by you, tell him what you want done he will tell you how wrong you are and how he don't need to do it that way. In the army we had a supply section where we were supposed to go for supplies. We all said it was the place you go and tell them what you needed and they would tell you how to get by without it, I just assumed that was their job, that was alright with me I could handle it, seems nobody on either side knows their perspective places, but I can assure you God knows his and yours and we might ought to learn them. God dwells a little more on the word responsibility than we do. We need to learn that God is not on the same level as we are, he is at the top and we need to communicate with him, as such. For it is plain that he will not bend himself to our level but will lift us up to him if we can study the word of God and put him in his perspective place, he has demanded it. I'll promise, you are missing life if you don't.

The problem is we think we can communicate with God on our

level but that is not possible and I don't know why we are so foolish as to think we can treat him like he is. He will not tolerate it and has told us so many times in his word that he won't. You start to read your Bible you will notice it starts out "In the beginning God...," And when we get to the end the first thing we will see is God. Even though we can't see him he is everything in between. So I would guess we all should establish a communication with him. They will not be all alike and will not have like assignments but we'll all be in one mind and one accord, one voice one judgment, can you imagine that happening? I can, but it will be the ones that will be with him for eternity, can you see now why he said there would be so few? I can, and it is scary, he told us to get ready down here you know. Like it or not, he is a spirit and them that worship him must worship him in spirit and truth. If you find another way please write a book to me about it, I'll be glad to read it. As I've already said God tried the patriarch, judges, prophets, priest and kings but men has not communicated with him or kept one of the many covenants they made with God and always went whoreing after other nations and gods, what do you think this nation is doing now?

His son volunteered to die for the few that he knew would except him. It pleased God, but God says tell them this is the last straw, they can accept this or else, there will be no other way offered. Jesus came for the lost sheep of Israel not us gentiles for we were alienated from God with no hope, but out of love for his creation Jesus made a way for us to be grafted in on the root which was him, Not for anything we have done, but for love he had for us he told his disciples you did not choose me, I chose you, if we don't except his way and love him more than our own life here and stay grafted into the root we are none of his, your choice. Again he says my yoke is easy and my burdens are light, but the way of a transgressor is hard.

We need never to put anything out in front of God or above God. He says to wait on him, we are to follow, not lead Jesus, and it is a disaster to ever put ourselves out before God or above him. Look at Job that story is there for our admonition and is schooling for anyone that can read and believe it, and is an example to anyone that wants to hear it correctly.

Job was a perfect man, nobody on earth like him, loved righteousness and hated evil. That was not good enough, he needed to repent and except a savior. He argued and stood on his own self-righteousness for thirty some odd chapters and had no presence of God available, he was beat down like no man I ever read about, everything Satan could produce short of death, he got so low his wife beg him to just curse God and die.

Job cursed the day he was born, asked God to just remove it from the calendar, but held onto his integrity and said he had committed no sin and had nothing to hide and beg for an audience with God and said he would come forth as fine gold when he could have his case heard but even if God slew him he would not give up his faith in God. His so called comforters kept telling him he was lying, admit it, for God would not allow that to be done, if he was not lying. In spite of all of the torcher his friends gave him, Job laid crowing like a fighting rooster till God showed up in a whirl wind, told Job to gird up his loins he was going to talk to him like a man. Why would he talk to him like anything else, he was a man. He ask who is this giving counsel without knowledge? Job saw God like he said he would, but he didn't have enough knowledge to answer one question of a hundred and sixty or so questions that God ask Job, about what Job knew about God. Job said, about as soon as he saw God, that he had been talking about things that was too great for him to know about and agreed to shut his mouth and listen to God.

Look how hard it is to get a perfect man to shut up and listen to God. I hope I'm not anywhere near as hard of hearing as that. God does know how to get your attention. It seems like the more self-righteous we get the harder it is for us to hear God. Reckon that might be the reason God doesn't like our self-righteousness. We cannot earn grace. Therefore salvation does not come by works or anything we can produce and certainly not by our looks or actions. God is not looking for people who act like Christians. He wants people that are Christians. If he was looking for actors I suppose he would set up his kingdom in Hollywood, I don't believe it is one of his favorite places, do you?

I'll ask around next time I'm out there, maybe I'll just look for him in some of the latest movies, I believe it would be hard to see him in very many of them, of course that's my opinion, but I'm willing to stand by it. God has promised that whosoever shall exalt himself will be abased and he that humbled himself shall be exalted in due time. Why don't we look at that saying for a little while, after all it is the Word of God and Jesus thundered all up through the Gospels for us to study the scriptures, they tell us of him, Son of God, and in essence everything. The word exalt means out or up in a spiritual sense. The word abase means to lower or put down, the opposite of exalt.

When man was determined to build a city against God, Babel, hence Babylon, God's defense was to scatter them throughout the world, to delay what mankind was determined to try do. Their reaction was for every man to take the spirit, or plan with him, conceived in his mind and to carry it out wherever he settled and to build his own Babylon city and name it after himself. Now this is hopelessness, by himself build apart from God but if they could unite into one, they thought they could build successfully and they could gain their independence and run the whole farm and reap all the harvest for themselves, I don't know why but the same spirit and problem exist today and the same situation, I can study all up through the history of man and still cannot explain why man is so determined to get free from God when God is the every ounce of life that he has in him, from anywhere. The only thing I can come up with, I reckon he just hates life itself. Now I know that there is them that have made great success and think they have found their life here and call that their religion and even enjoying gloating in their pride and success and learned to put on a happy face but them kind cannot acknowledge the Bible or the Lord Jesus Christ as their savior or the God of the Bible for they all condemn them to hell from one end to the other. They can never create an everlasting life anywhere in all the technology that man has acquired, even though he has tried since he was created.

God says he hates a proud look. I wonder what he thinks of that look that Obama loves to pose in. Jesus says if you find your life here you will lose it when you get over there. I could fill my book with condemnation on them but since they do not believe the Bible it would be futile.

When God scattered the men he sure knew what he was doing. A few thousand years later and he has not only, not pulled himself together, but is farther apart than he has ever been. The reason being, to unite into one requires a head. With everybody having a desire to be the head, or control of the head, or by killing, stealing, destroying, clawing and scratching their way to the closest spot to the head as possible, never being content with any position short of the head itself seems to create a battling situation. There is only one person in God's creation that can be that head, and he will be, when this thing plays out, which it is going to. It happens to be The Lord Jesus Christ, the only one with anything eternal, including life, the only begotten son of God. There is not another name under heaven by which men must be saved by.

Without God, the only righteous one, at the head there is only one situation left, confusion, chaos, called dog eat dog, or a rat race, or one of the other such names that man has given it. I think God called it hell and covered it pretty well. It is the condition the world is in today and getting worse and worse, faster and faster, and if you think it's going to turn around and get any better, even for a short time, I think you are thinking like a fool and apparently have not read where Jesus said plainly that it would wax worse and worse.

God set a precedence for the world and ever smart man, or foolish man, owing to which direction you are looking at it from, thinking he is the one that should be setting in the seat of God, since they cannot see God they think everybody has the same opportunity to attain the seat, act like God, divide and conquer and destroy everything that opposes him. Well, that is the way it is done and the way it is going to be done, but God says there is only one God, there was no god here when I came, there is no god here with me now, and there will be no gods here when I'm gone, I believe that about covers it. The desire of man to be that head has created that seven headed beast that Daniel and John saw and the other prophets told so much about, that rose up out of the sea of humanity. God has told us so much about this beast, even a few thousand years ago. It is still growing and operating well, till today. God has never missed pronounced a fact about it yet. One of them being that it has not acquired one eternal thing yet and is never going too apart from God. And even most preachers cannot see it yet, and it has been running the world for well over three thousand years, and we think Jesus is lying when he told us how blind we are, and so much about it, and about his kingdom two thousand years ago, and I don't know of one lie yet that men has been able to expose. Some people have got their nerve, I'd say millions of people have been destroyed way before their time for lying to and lying about God and never had a clue, they could have understood it well if they would have just read their Bible with a little understanding.

Before you start judging me and pointing all your fingers at me to tear me down to justify yourself, I might say to start with, you can't justify yourself for eating your breakfast this morning. Jesus is the only justifier, we have no one else, and no one else is needed, and I have no intention of judging, accusing, blaming, or condemning anybody. God has told each of us to judge ourselves and he want have to judge us. I cannot judge a sand flea, I cannot hurt you in any way in judgment, and neither can you hurt me. But I can tell you an old saying that is much older than me, "if the shoe fits you will wear it," I have nothing to do with that saying just heard it and saw it all my life.

I've tried to put as much in this book about judging as I feel led to, it must be about the most abused and misused word in the Bible, as I have said before in here it could sure do for a lot of studying by anybody. And it will be about the most important moment you will have to encounter, take my word for it. God has told us so much about this seven headed kingdom that will only be totally destroyed in the last war and judgment. It is operative till today but cannot succeed because it is still scatted and cannot pull itself together under one head because nobody can serve two masters, no two people can be the head, one has to kill the other in order to be one head by himself, so as long as there is two men left alive, each one is trying to kill the other to get the head spot. Can you solve that problem? God can, and has already told us how he is going to do it, every man must die. He has given us a lifetime to get ready. He even told us many ways to prolong our life to get prepared for it. He is going to destroy all flesh, all mankind, all his inventions, all his great ideas along with the heaven and earth that man has polluted, and start all over with a few that have made themselves righteous through the blood of his son Jesus Christ and loves it. Among one of the last things Jesus said to us in the Bible was, "behold, I make all things new." After saying "the words I speak they are spirit and they are life." I believe God has assured me that he will keep me going till I finish this book and in some form or another, he will. I've said this to a few people when I started out on it, all came back with a similar reply, one said you ought to take at least 10 years to finish it, another, I believe I would take a 100 years or so to finish it. I thought foolish, I'm not of that mind or spirit at all, for I know you can never get away from God even by dying or making your place among the stars or in the pits of hell, for he knows all about both places and told us so, he always knows where we are, and we can never manipulate or use him, he will not allow that to happen, even if he calls me, cannot he say well you finished didn't you? I intend to make a small point with this story, now I intended no reflection on the guys that answered me or to myself other than we're just people, and very common at that. The guys did not know the whole story.

My age and miles are catching up with me and I was feeling sort of sorry for myself and was talking to God about maybe just taking me home, like a shortcut or something, I think maybe I was looking more for pity than death, I don't know, I was talking to him about it. I really had not thought seriously about writing a book. But God started telling me a few things, like I was going to write a book, and he was going to keep me going till I got it done. So I wasn't really interested in prolonging my time and decided I needed to get it going. I sure didn't want to be wrong about the rapture and fool around and miss it for not finishing a work that God told me that I was going to have to finish before he would let me come home so I been burning the midnight oil for I want to be ready, it is the kind of spirit I have and think God for it.

Yet people on every corner will try to out figure God, it is useless,

I've got so much I could write here, I'm almost lost, some could come under the heading of, don't get yourself in front of God, or grab yourself a skate board, that is one I've been given much on, one is on spirit you are of. I'll start toward it.

I sat under a pasture that was easy to get fired up and easy to get carried away with any big idea that sounded good, especially if he came up with it, he called it an anointing, I wondered. Someone without a little spiritual discernment can get himself into deep water in a hurry, if he is not cautious. Most call it an attitude some might call it a nature or ego maybe any one of a dozen other carnal names, I could not find the word attitude in my Bible, so I began a study to see what the Bible used for a substitute, a word used as much by us as attitude had to have a substitute in God's dictionary, I came up with, "the spirit you are of," that was some years ago, and I've grew stronger on it ever since, so when someone has a bad attitude, he is in a bad spirit, he needs to get a spirit adjustment, not an attitude adjustment. It is much easier to change the spirit that you have than to change your carnal temper, anger and nervous breakdown feelings that the more you cater to, the bigger and stronger they get. Because they are of a carnal spirit and are contrary to the spirit of God. As long as you put up with them the more in control they will get and soon they will have to put you in a strait jacket if you're not careful. You change the spirit you are of and you will have a different attitude.

This is why it is so important to know the spirit you are of, and to know the spirit you are dealing with. It can and will change your very life, if you can learn what God meant when he said his people will be minding the things of the spirit, not the things of the flesh. It will change a nation and a nation can change the world. Anybody interested in trying it?

I reckon the Christians of today are satisfied with the world of today. They sure act like it, but let me give you a little warning. God said he was on the verge of doing something about that. We will see how that works out, if we hang around long enough.

God says he will plead with us with his wrath, the mother of harlots and abomination of this world church has already built us a wall around all that, called the rapture. I'm told to pray to be found worthy to escape that, and stand before the Lord Jesus. Well I'm confident that is exactly where I am standing. I cannot recall all the times I've been rebuked with, well when Jesus comes, my feet is leaving this earth, I'm going to be taken out of here, into what?

Space I reckon, they can't show me anywhere else, except a comet or meteor, my question is, what is so assuring about their feet leaving the ground, what are they going to need them for, out in space, maybe to run on, from one cloud to another, or maybe to catch up to a comet for a ride. I decided some time ago, when Jesus decides to catch me up unto himself he can do whatever he wants to do with these old wore out, fleshly, earthy feet, I do not need them anymore, I'm going to be trying out my whole new body I'm promised. Where is their faith? Where is their spiritual mind, seems like they lost it if they ever had one. If they don't get out of that carnal mind and quit trying to measure and judge everybody but themselves. They do not have any spirit of God in them. If they don't have no spirit in them, then they are none of his, then they will not have on the proper wedding garment, they will be bound hand and foot and cast into outer darkness.

I'm sure their feet will still be left on them because they were bound, maybe this is the rapture they are preaching about it's the closest thing I can find in scripture to the thing they are preaching. The Bible is spiritually written and spiritually discerned, the carnal does not know one thing about the spirit, there is nothing about the rapture they teach that I see is spiritual, They try to explain everything about it with carnal reasoning they don't need a Bible to do that, just a carnal mind. There is not going to be one carnal mind going to make it into Jesus Christ's body in any form, at any time, so why try to hang onto it when it is sure death, if we are not born into the spirit of God and walking in the spirit, God says you are not one of his. Now if you cannot know the spirit you are of, and the spirit you are talking to, how can you say you know the spirit of God? If you don't know and learn the spirit you are of, Jesus says you are blind and cannot see, deaf and can't hear, and void of any understanding. And If you don't like it, let Jesus know about it the next time you talk to him. He said it, I didn't, but I can read it to you, if you cannot find it in your Bible, or have trouble reading. Back to the preacher I mentioned, that was easy to get fired up, he called it an anointing, I wondered, but he was frequently saying, "you do this,. you do that, you obligate God." I'd about melt in my seat, I could not phantom a man that could obligate God, that was thirty some odd years ago and I still cannot visualize such a creature in my wildest imagination, even until today.

I suppose writers of star wars or star track could vision such a thing and make it seem real, but I think God I don't have such a mind and would not want to send it there if I did. I am neither envious nor jealous of them that can and do, just not very interested. I would not want to be a man that could manipulate God, or set in his seat for him, I'm sure I'm enough human, that sooner or later I'd start telling myself I was God. That is the spirit of a human, the spirit of the world, and the spirit of antichrist.

Jesus was given all power on heaven and earth, after the resurrection and is setting at the right hand of the father today and I can assure you that he has never entertained the thought of killing the Father in order to move over into his seat, he said the Father is greater than me and he is happy to be equal with the father and be one with him. But man is not happy to be counted equal with Jesus and be counted sons and daughters of God, and one with Christ Jesus. Read all about it in your Bible and see if it is not all right there before us, for the taking if we can just believe and trust God enough to act upon it. If not, there is nothing left for you but death, the second death, or eternal death. Is not the creation you are setting in enough to convince you? He has even invited us to try it, taste and see if it isn't so, prove him, he says.

Now that doesn't mean inquire of him, I believe maybe every man alive has inquired of God, Saul for an example, the Bible says he enquired of God and God did not answer him, neither by prophet or by dream. Samuel, who he quite listening to died and Saul was lost again, so he went looking for a witch for guidance.

He had to go completely out of Israel to find one for he had killed all the witches in God's kingdom on God's orders. He found a witch who obeyed him after he promised protection to her, she called up Samuel who told him he would be dead tomorrow, and he was. God said Saul perished because he sought a witch instead of God. That put some distance between enquiring and seeking.

He said for us to taste and see, I believe that implies seeking and sampling, now don't you? You can keep in mind God said he would give us the desires of our hearts if we sought long enough, but he did not add to that, only if it is good for you, so be careful what you desire, God said a heart is deceiving above anything, so don't follow your heart if it is not being led by the light of the Gospel and the mind of Christ. For your feelings are usually country miles from walking with God's spirit. God also says if your heart condemns you God's word is greater.

It may grieve our spirit but it will never grieve God's spirit, which he told us not to do. And if we are not looking up and forward, and walking in the spirit of God as he said to walk, then we are not looking where we are walking. The spirit of God is always moving, but since God don't always see moving or direction as our carnal minds sees, then this is where we need to put aside carnal minds, and hop onto the spiritual wagon that is always moving in the right direction. If you don't it will just pass you right on by, you will be left behind, the time is now and we never know how long now is going to last. We are not guaranteed another minute, of course we are all expecting to last for a lot longer. We live by hope but we are all guaranteed that time will end. I know this is put fairly straight but I hope there are a few people that will read this and not be like so many I have met, including my own blood brother, told me you're my brother and I reckon I love you, but I just can't stand your preaching. He is a book and seminary trained Assembly of God preacher and pasture teacher.

Others have told me the same thing in different ways, I'm sorry for their pain, but I see nothing I've said that I feel I need to apologize for, and I've gotten used to being rejected and criticized, after close to forty years of it, but I have no intention to quit. My preaching is not wrapped up in my feelings so they don't matter that much, but if you can show me from the word of God some place I am wrong.

I will thank you big time and will try vigorously to correct myself. Because as I heard Glenn Beck say, opinions should cease when truth is presented.

Speaking of rejection and Glenn Beck, I recently talked to a man and the name Sean Hannity came up and he let out a line about how stupid and sorry and crazy Hannity was, then ask if that was the one on TV with Colmbs, I said yes, he was the one with Hannity and Colmbs a few years ago. He says, well he didn't watch TV any more it's nothing but lies. Well I would almost agree with him and a few churches I know that forbid their congregation to have a TV in their house, but not completely. I've told all of them that could hear, I could preach against what comes on TV for the rest of my life and probably will, but what good would it do to preach against the TV itself, maybe ask God to smash the screen in on every TV I look at? Would that make me look like a righteous man of God to these people and churches I just mentioned? I am likely going to mention a few more times, just stay tuned if you can stand it.

Just for an add on, I've heard my brother, I just mentioned, say a lot of the same things about poor old Hannity. It's not just about Hannity, it's about all Christians, and Glenn Beck is out in front of Hannity so he takes more rejection than Hannity and I combined. I had a man to get right into my face, telling me I was the stupidest person that he ever had to talk to, because I said I thought Glenn Beck was a Christian. He was telling me, he could not be a Christian for he was a Mormon and a Mormon believes "such and such" and could not be a Christian. I stated, I had never heard Glen say that he was a Mormon, and we had no authority to judge a man to say if he was a Christian or not, that's when he went off on me, said that he had heard him say it, and he had the right to know, preached himself into a frenzy, and said them big words about me. He finally got up, preached himself out the door, quit his job and left the recording studio owner and me to finish the session. Next day he called the radio station that plays my little preaching skit each week and complained that he thought he ought not to put me on the air for he had heard me say things that was not lawful. This man was a minister too. My point is that it is getting to where it is not safe to stand up for a Christian, while others are making millions for bashing them. The laws for separation of church and state, and you cannot say the name Jesus in a government school Christmas play, or graduation, sets up a perfect scene to play out this kind of results. Jesus talked about people being blind and having ears but couldn't hear, he was not talking about the heathen, they are dead, he was talking to and about God's people, so called, Christians of today, and if they cannot see and hear what I've been talking about, and then I know real well what Jesus was talking about. If you cannot, he is saying you are dead, or deaf and blind. Ever notice how quick they will defend the lawmen and judges that slay these people that do stand up for Christians, that makes them popular and profitable and in high standing with the world, and even with other so called Christians, and Christians cannot see which side they are on? Or as I say what spirit they are of. Reckon that might be a little of what God was talking about, like blind leading the blind and they will both fall in the ditch.

The farther you dig the deeper it gets. Maybe I should go to something else. The man that preached himself out the door, I was told a little later, he lost his position in the place where he worked on his real job and moved to another and later I heard he walked off his job altogether for no more of a reason than you have heard here. The guy has problems but it isn't very smart to take them up with God. He didn't know that just a few months before some preachers had come together and preached across the country against them lying, political correct, God hating, antichrist, government worshiping, demon possessed, liberals, and succeeded in pushing them back a little and gained a lot of liberty for a lot of little preachers like myself, if we can move up into it, instead of joining them antichrist zealots and attacking them like Hannity and Beck. Two of the better Christians that I know of, they are on our side, if some of these blind people can see it or not. It will not be up to them to judge our reward them in any way.

I am so glad of that. I know Glenn Beck is a man of God for God told me so, about the second are third time I saw him on tv some years ago and we have had a spiritual relationship ever since, even though he don't know me from Adam and I've never met him are spoke to him. You have to be questioning, how can that be? If you are not spiritual, you could never know, and I will not try to explain it to you for it would sound too much like I was trying to glory myself.

I don't want to even sound like it and give all of you occasion to attack me. I get enough attacks as it is, without inviting more. Not that I can't handle them, but you would be trying to stop the word of God going forth, just like all them people I've been talking about, and I do not want to help you do it, you can do that at your own risk, that is God's department, not mine. I make a special effort to not covet God's seat, I know that belongs to him and I'm confident that he can handle it very well without my help and if he needs me to stand for him he'll let me know. I hope I can say here I am, and mean it.

Of course I have not been asked to, but my confidence in Glenn Beck's position and standing with God is strong enough, that if necessary, I would stake my life on it. So it gets under my righteous indignation, (if there is such a thing) to hear someone speak such lying judgmental remarks, from such ignorance and lack of knowledge about such people., or any people.

But you can hear it almost in a constant flow, for the world never runs into short supply of such mouths. I suppose they have a better supply section than we had when I worked for the army in the 1950's. This country has been so educated against God, that if a politician mentions God he can just about forget getting elected to a public office.

God didn't destroy carnality completely in the days of Noah, but saved eight souls and an ark full of animals. I don't believe God saved every species of animals on the Earth, just the ones that obeyed him and reported to Noah, and loaded on the ark. And he well knew the ones he wanted.

We've elected just enough God fearing people to Washington DC to pull us up out of the depressions that the same people will drive us back into, after blaming the ones that pulled us out for the things they just pulled us out of, then getting enough elected to tear it back down again in two turns of blaming it on the ones that pulled it out the last time. This has been going on since they dropped the country on Hoover and put the great Federal Reserve System into effect and raised the country back up a little with a world war and fulfilled his prophecy to set Israel back in its own country. God said in his word that it was just a little thing to him, that he blessed us and raised us up to do that, but we thought we took God's seat clean out from under him and no longer needed him for anything, so we are throwing him out of the way of our government. We don't believe that he has any power, most don't believe he even exist, almost no one believes he created us all, they teach that we evolved by eons of time from water running over a rock. They don't know where the water and the rock came from, their still working on that, but I'm sure they will come up with the answer. I suspect they will have to add our age up into the trillions of years since time is the only thing they can come up with to find creative power. I still have not figured out where it is at in time, but who am I to question a scientist with intelligence above God, completely out of our sight. (Me and God)

So congress, with its gay groups, something for nothing groups, separate from God groups, illegal alien groups, minority groups, black groups, saying the republicans have been trying to put them back into slavery ever since they defeated the Democrats in the civil war and freed the slaves, I'm having a hard time understanding that, but I reckon everybody believes it, especially the blacks, course Jessie Jackson and Al Sharpton have been, and are still being paid millions and millions of dollars to keep the blacks believing that, and believing the republicans are declaring war on the old people, the aliens, the women, the unions, I'm getting tired naming them, you name a few and I'll guarantee the Democrats will put their name to it that the Republicans have declared war on them, and if you can sell it for them they will pay you a few million, they don't care about the cost, you name your price as long as you produce, they have an endless supply of money as long as they can keep on being elected for they are spending the taxpayers money, and China and Japan is backing their credit card. Can you beat that? Looks like a perfect plan to me.

Do you reckon I might get a job with them Democrats? No, too many already got their application in before me, everybody wants to be a Democrat, or at least on the payroll.

If you hear of me being gathered up off of a rail road track, and their medical examiner declares me to have been out and asleep on marijuana and on the rail road track, just a few facts I might state here. I've not only never inhaled, I've never took a draw off of marijuana, I've never laid down to sleep on a rail road track, and foresee no such event. But if they can put enough of my face back together and look real close they can probably see that I am smiling. I am 74 years old and lived a full and complete life and said about everything I felt a need to say, and know my savior, so it will be hard for them to take very much away from me.

Washington D.C. and its God hating, something for nothing, gay groups has outlawed opening your mouth about anything about Jesus Christ, making it a criminal offence, the so called Christians loving it, because someone calling himself a Baptist cannot teach my child, which is a Pentecostal, one word about Jesus. While homosexuals can teach both, all about how to live man with man, women with women, and Christians of course cannot see a thing wrong with that as long as they don't put a religious name on it you can teach anything to them that our good old wise government approves, while the 17th chapter of the book of revelation church, the beast rider, the mother of harlots and abominations of the world is running our government. I'm sure God will reward you for giving your kids such protection, as a rapture theory and a denomination name, which should really have them protected against any wrath God could pour out.

We have one protection against God's wrath, the same righteous one we have had from the beginning, the righteous garment of the lord Jesus Christ, and if you're not wearing it, you will be standing naked before God and I don't believe he is going to like what he sees, at least he says he won't.

I guess you might be worshiping O'Rilley's god that doesn't know how to write a book that you can go to, for truth, or Goldburg's god that knows how old God's creation is, when our God missed it by

a few billion years. Guess God must have been asleep, those few billion years, reckon he will be mad at them for knowing all about these things and not waking him up. Sure glad I'm not O'Rilley, or Goldburg, I bet they will at least get a scolding. Congress's laws, so foolish as to make it a crime, to mention the Bible or Jesus Christ, or displaying anything crossed on government property and will be deported if they want to teach their children that we have such liberty.

It's ok for an illegal alien to get drunk, run down innocent Citizens, he will be given a citizenship and a job, receive SS and SSI the only difference I can see is the one wanted to teach was a Christian, the one wanted to kill was going to vote Democrat. I really don't want to blame congressmen, they've chose their heaven right here on this earth, but I believe that God has reserved a special place in hell for people who voted for them and claimed to be Christians. They would have to be literally deaf and blind or willingly ignorant to not know what they were voting for. Just in case they still don't know what they voted for I will tell them, they voted their selfish, greedy, lustful, envious, self-interest. No interest in another human being's fillings unless they were identical to their own immoral God hating feelings. It's no marvel that God said so many times for his people to wake up out of sleep and stand up for him and be counted on his side and be seen, or we are not on his side. Again Jesus said he did not come to bring peace, but division. Most Christians I know think that is just another misprint in the Bible that Jesus said to study. Those wanting to be the head against God, I've been writing about has divided billions of people and gotten hundreds of millions of people killed in the short 6000 years God has given us in time to live on his creation, and promised us it will get much worse before this last 1000 years is finished. Which side are you on? I keep forgetting O'Rilly and Goldburg says, the Bible is not true, and they have a lot of followers, look at the people that has tried to rewrite it, but God ask, "What can you add to the perfect?"